Social Studies Plus!
A Hands-On Approach

Editorial Offices: Glenview, Illinois • Parsippany, New Jersey • New York, New York
Sales Offices: Parsippany, New Jersey • Duluth, Georgia • Glenview, Illinois •
Coppell, Texas • Ontario, California

www.sfsocialstudies.com

Program Authors

Dr. Candy Dawson Boyd
Professor, School of Education
Director of Reading Programs
St. Mary's College
Moraga, California

Dr. Geneva Gay
Professor of Education
University of Washington
Seattle, Washington

Rita Geiger
Director of Social Studies and
    Foreign Languages
Norman Public Schools
Norman, Oklahoma

Dr. James B. Kracht
Associate Dean for
    Undergraduate Programs
    and Teacher Education
College of Education
Texas A&M University
College Station, Texas

Dr. Valerie Ooka Pang
Professor of Teacher Education
San Diego State University
San Diego, California

Dr. C. Frederick Risinger
Director, Professional
    Development and Social
    Studies Education
Indiana University
Bloomington, Indiana

Sara Miranda Sanchez
Elementary and Early
    Childhood Curriculum
    Coordinator
Albuquerque Public Schools
Albuquerque, New Mexico

Contributing Authors

Dr. Carol Berkin
Professor of History
Baruch College and the
    Graduate Center
The City University of New York
New York, New York

Lee A. Chase
Staff Development Specialist
Chesterfield County
    Public Schools
Chesterfield County, Virginia

Dr. Jim Cummins
Professor of Curriculum
Ontario Institute for Studies
    in Education
University of Toronto
Toronto, Canada

Dr. Allen D. Glenn
Professor and Dean Emeritus
Curriculum and Instruction
College of Education
University of Washington
Seattle, Washington

Dr. Carole L. Hahn
Professor, Educational Studies
Emory University
Atlanta, Georgia

Dr. M. Gail Hickey
Professor of Education
Indiana University-Purdue
    University
Fort Wayne, Indiana

Dr. Bonnie Meszaros
Associate Director
Center for Economic Education
    and Entrepreneurship
University of Delaware
Newark, Delaware

ISBN: 0-328-03595-5

12 13 14 15 16 DBH 10 09

Contents

Contents

Welcome to *Social Studies Plus!*

Using Activities to Launch Social Studies Classes

Most educators are all too familiar with the "banking" metaphor of learning, where students sit passively as receivers of information. Educators also know the need to switch that construct to a vital one where students *participate* in the wide world that social studies class can reveal. To jump-start this new metaphor, it helps to have a variety of dynamic and broad-range activities that draw life and direction from the content and skills of basic social studies curriculum. In this way, students begin to realize that the issues of social studies concern things they care about.

Social studies, of course, is about both the forest and the trees. It covers the whole world—big and little events, heroes and ordinary people, issues of justice, morality, and ethics. Social studies is also about the *specific*—the content and skills connected with historical fact and assessing controversial issues that students learn to work with at their own levels of understanding.

When we teach social studies, it is important to join all the important historical, political, and economic aspects of the curriculum with the concrete ways students learn and express themselves. It makes sense, then, to engage students in many different kinds of activities so as to appeal to the varied ways students tackle any curriculum but especially the broad curriculum of social studies. A variety of approaches helps students internalize what citizenship means and how important participation is for a democracy to thrive.

Social Studies Plus! Overview and Purpose

Social Studies Plus! begins with Scott Foresman's social studies basal scope and sequence and then sets up engaging activities that invite students to think independently about events and issues in both the past and present. Some activities create a storytelling atmosphere, where students can move from the concrete to the abstract. Some *Social Studies Plus!* activities place the student in the middle of an historical event and ask the student to take a position and justify it. Other activities promote discussion, questioning, and analysis about the consequences resulting from events, ideas, and persons' actions. Not only should the ideas presented open students' thinking and get them interested in social studies curriculum, the activities should also help students see that they have something at stake in the issues of being a citizen.

Social Studies Plus! offers several approaches in which students may participate:

- Students may create simulations by playing various roles; for instance, they may become members of an immigrant family arriving at Ellis Island, or they may act out the parts of weary soldiers at Valley Forge under General George Washington.

- Students may dig into hands-on activities by drawing themselves on "living" time lines as characters in the early colonies or on the Underground Railroad.

- Students may use their math and graphic organizer skills to map out or graph the fast clip of progress during the Industrial Revolution.

- Students may design labor union broadsides or cartoons about the 1920s, which then may trigger critical discussions of moral and ethical issues.

- Some students may use biographical sketches of famous people in history to stimulate their own writing of persuasive speeches, poems, or news articles that show a variety of perspectives.

Each unit follows a basic progression. First, a Long-Term Project presents a unit theme for students to work on throughout the study of the unit. Second, other unit themes are presented in creative and dramatic form in a six-page Drama section. Third, a number of Short-Term Projects, Writing Projects, and Citizenship activities further develop the topics covered in each chapter.

Read ahead to see how each unit is mapped out and how to make the most of all the projects and activities presented in *Social Studies Plus!*

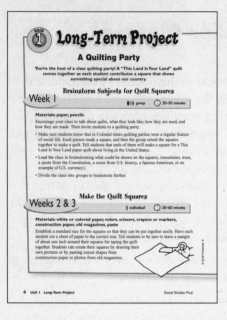

Long-Term Project

Students are offered a Long-Term Project that may last several days or weeks. The goal of the project is to extend the main ideas of an entire unit and allow students enough time to perform one or several tasks. For instance, students may draw, make graphs, do an interview, or complete some research on one topic. With the Long-Term Project, students have time to enter into the discussion of an issue, or they launch into making something concrete, such as a model, diorama, puppets, and so on. The unit project, then, allows students to integrate key social studies concepts and skills in an organized, and often artistic, way.

These unit-sized projects may suggest that the teacher set the context or recall topics at hand, or the teacher may choose how much background to give students. Students do not always need prior experience with the topics presented. Procedures for handling the project are laid out in easy-to-follow steps where teachers may choose the grouping and specific tasks so that, by unit's end, everyone contributes to an overall display or project. Students usually end up choosing what goes into a report or display, allowing them the chance to *own* a part of the display. One of the most enlightening parts of the unit project happens when students present their endeavors to one another or to other classes. A close second to that experience occurs when their audiences ask the students questions and the students become experts for the moment.

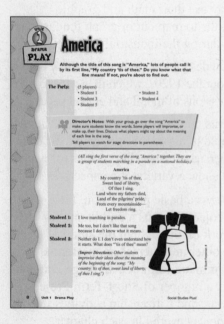

Drama: Plays

Every activity in the Drama section of *Social Studies Plus!* is aimed at creating a dramatic and physical reaction in students to some social studies issues. All the activities give students opportunities for improvising.

The plays are presented either as fully written scripts or as plays with some written lines and suggested ways for improvising additional lines and scenes. In addition, most plays are based on the following parameters:

- The plays take no longer than 30–40 minutes at a time, although play practice and presentation may extend over several class periods.

- The plays are appropriate for each age group in both dialogue and plot complexity.

- The plays are accompanied by a director's guide that will help the student-leader or teacher by providing plot summary, prop and theater term suggestions, or character descriptions.

Drama: Scenarios

Scenarios give students the opportunity to act out brief scenes that draw on their spur-of-the-moment reactions as well as promote their abilities to think on their feet. These scenarios relate to the topics and skills at hand and do not require outside research. Each scenario will:

• provide students with a purpose and focus for the scenario,

• often suggest a conflict relevant to the students' life experiences,

• be easily done in the classroom with a few optional props,

• take only about 10–15 minutes to present,

• and often allow students opportunities to think beyond their usual perspective about facts and people.

There are several common theater terms used throughout the Drama section. See the glossary on page 1 for a full set of theater terms. You may want to copy the page and make it available to the students.

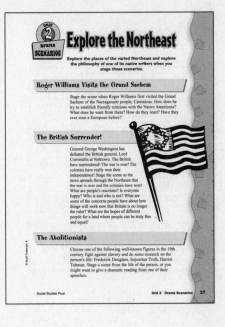

Chapter Development

Short-Term Projects

The goal of the many Short-Term Projects is to extend the chapter content. No projects are repeated from the Teacher's Edition. Rather they proceed from the themes and topics of interest in the Student's Edition and so allow students a myriad of hands-on activities. These projects are oriented toward engaging students in the following ways:

• Short-Term Projects engage small groups, partners, individuals or the whole class in relevant activities.

• They encompass a wide variety of activities: map making, debates, theme mobiles, banners and collages, speeches, time lines from Ancient Egypt to the town of Egypt, Maine, and many more.

• They suggest ways for the students to have fun with social studies topics and skills.

• They cover skills to help students think "out of the box."

• They offer directions that students may follow without much adult assistance.

• They integrate various subject areas into a social studies project.

• They can be completed in about 20–30 minutes.

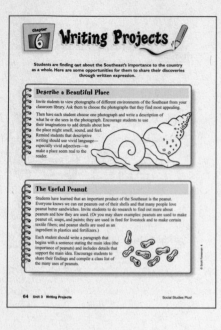

Writing Projects

In a grab bag approach, some Writing Projects allow a wide swath of creativity and some take students through brief, but rigorous, expository writing. The Writing Projects should also include the following goals.

- The Writing Projects engage students in a variety of dynamic writing applications of social studies content and skills and can be completed in about 20–30 minutes.

- They serve as a bridge between students' (a) prior knowledge and life experiences and (b) content of the core text.

- They provide a connection between concrete/operational understanding and the application of social studies concepts/skills to a student's life.

- They should help students experience social studies in ways other than rehashing dates and events.

- They should be intriguing enough to make teachers and students *both* want to try the activities.

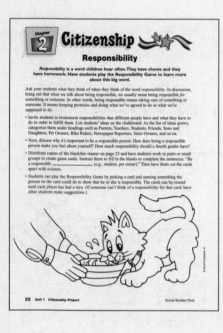

Citizenship

Social studies always deals with citizens of the past and present. To show students how important participation is in a democratic society, these activities focus on the traits of a good citizen.

- Each Citizenship page may require some research, creative writing, interviews, or artistic endeavors.

- The goal of this page is to make students more aware of how to spot citizenship traits in their own actions and in the larger neighborhood or community around them.

Blackline Masters

Each chapter has at least one blackline master for students to use to further extend one or more of the activities in the unit or chapter. Some of these pages engage students in crossword puzzles, cartoon strips and storyboards, graphic organizers, map and graph making, and various kinds of artwork.

Assessment for *Social Studies Plus!*

The rubrics suggested for use with *Social Studies Plus!* materials are intended to aid teachers in recording a range of the students' linguistic and cultural experiences.

The emphasis of these rubrics is placed on thinking rather than rote learning, performance and successes rather than failings, and on each individual's development within grade-level expectations. Obviously no rubrics are a substitute for the teacher's classroom observations. A teacher's notes on students' abilities to gain knowledge based on experience is key in helping teachers make students understand what they need to learn.

The rubrics presented in *Social Studies Plus!* pertain to assessing students' achievements while they are engaged in exploring the social studies content and learning new skills. Applying these rubrics to the students' work gives them concrete feedback and helps them monitor their own progress toward meeting performance standards. These rubrics are oriented toward assessing the variety of ways students may approach the content and skills of this program.

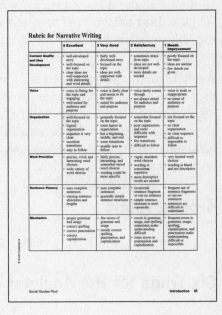

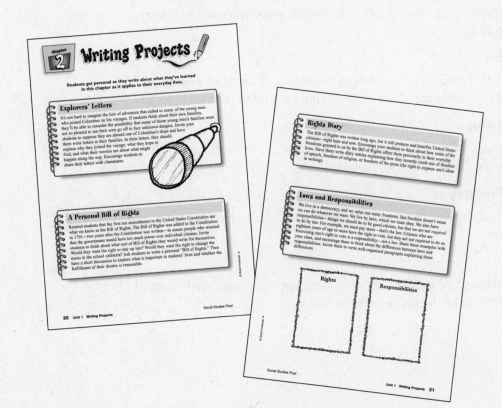

Writing Rubrics

Writing, because it is specific and tangible, may be easier to evaluate than most other subjects. Both analytic and holistic rubrics are used to evaluate writing. Many teachers use holistic scoring because it evaluates a writer's overall ability to express meaning in written form.

Analytic rubrics tend to incorporate spelling, punctuation, and grammar accuracy, yet they also address some complex aspects of writing assessment. This rubric is based on the assumption that teachers will be looking at students' abilities to begin handling some stages of the writing process in relation to social studies content. Once students have some specific ideas of how to improve their writing, they can begin to be their own editors.

4-point rubric

4 Excellent   **3** Very Good   **2** Satisfactory   **1** Needs Improvement

Six Traits for the Analytic Writing Rubric

Content Quality and Idea Development

genre well controlled, interesting, clear, complex, organized, details in place

Voice

specific, honest, appealing, clear point of view, appropriate use of action verbs, easy to follow

Organization

complete text, details in place, smooth transitions, fluency of thought, builds anticipation, creates interest, contains beginning, middle, and end

Word Precision

interesting, precise, and vivid word choice, strong verbs, understands appropriate phrasing, handles repairs well

Sentence Fluency

variation in sentence structure and length, uses sentence patterns when appropriate

Mechanics

correct grammar and spelling, sensible paragraphing, formal and informal punctuation used appropriately, easy to read

Rubric for Narrative Writing

	4 Excellent	3 Very Good	2 Satisfactory	1 Needs Improvement
Content Quality and Idea Development	• well-developed story • well-focused on the topic • clear ideas are well-supported with interesting and vivid details	• fairly well-developed story • focused on the topic • ideas are well-supported with details	• sometimes strays from topic • ideas are not well-developed • more details are needed	• poorly focused on the topic • ideas are unclear • few details are given
Voice	• voice is fitting for the topic and engaging • well-suited for audience and purpose	• voice is fairly clear and seems to fit the topic • suited for audience and purpose	• voice rarely comes through • not always suited for audience and purpose	• voice is weak or inappropriate • no sense of audience or purpose
Organization	• well-focused on the topic • logical organization • sequence is very clear • excellent transitions • easy to follow	• generally focused on the topic • some lapses in organization • has a beginning, middle, and end • some transitions • usually easy to follow	• somewhat focused on the topic • poor organization and some difficulty with sequence • few transitions • difficult to follow	• not focused on the topic • no clear organization • no clear sequence • difficult to impossible to follow
Word Precision	• precise, vivid, and interesting word choices • wide variety of word choices	• fairly precise, interesting, and somewhat varied word choices • wording could be more specific	• vague, mundane word choices • wording is sometimes repetitive • more descriptive words are needed	• very limited word choices • wording is bland and not descriptive
Sentence Fluency	• uses complete sentences • varying sentence structures and lengths	• uses complete sentences • generally simple sentence structures	• occasional sentence fragment or run-on sentence • simple sentence structure is used repeatedly	• frequent use of sentence fragments or run-on sentences • sentences are difficult to understand
Mechanics	• proper grammar and usage • correct spelling • correct punctuation • correct capitalization	• few errors of grammar and usage • mostly correct spelling, punctuation, and capitalization	• errors in grammar, usage, and spelling sometimes make understanding difficult • some errors in punctuation and capitalization	• frequent errors in grammar, usage, spelling, capitalization, and punctuation make understanding difficult or impossible

Rubric for Persuasive Writing

	4 Excellent	3 Very Good	2 Satisfactory	1 Needs Improvement
Content Quality and Idea Development	• clear position is well-supported and insightful • complete control of topic • many facts and opinions to support position • presents a convincing argument	• clear position is somewhat supported • good control of topic • some facts and opinions to support position • presents a fairly convincing argument	• position is taken, but not supported • some control of topic • few facts and opinions to support position • presents a weak argument	• no clear position taken • little control of topic • no facts and opinions given • no argument presented
Voice	• voice is strong and engaging • specific, honest, engaging point of view • well-suited for audience and purpose	• voice is fairly strong • generally clear, honest, engaging point of view • suited for audience and purpose	• voice rarely comes through • general, vague discussion of topic • not always suited for audience and purpose	• voice is weak or inappropriate • no particular point of view presented • no sense of audience or purpose
Organization	• well-focused on the topic • logical organization with reasons presented in a clear order • contains beginning, middle, and end • easy to follow argument	• generally focused on the topic • organization is mostly clear but reasons not always presented in a clear order • contains beginning, middle, and end • usually easy to follow argument	• somewhat focused on the topic • poor organization with only a few reasons presented • no clear beginning, middle, and end • difficult to follow argument	• not focused on the topic • no clear organization • no reasons presented • no clear beginning, middle, and end • no argument presented
Word Precision	• precise, persuasive word choices • interesting word choice • fluency of thought • appropriate use of action verbs	• fairly precise, persuasive word choices • wording could be more specific • generally appropriate use of action verbs	• vague, unpersuasive word choices • wording is general and not convincing • wording is sometimes repetitive	• very limited word choices • fails to persuade • wording is redundant and bland
Sentence Fluency	• uses complete sentences • varying sentence structures and lengths	• uses complete sentences • generally simple sentence structures	• occasional sentence fragment or run-on sentence • simple sentence structure is used repeatedly	• frequent use of sentence fragments or run-on sentences • sentences are difficult to understand
Mechanics	• proper grammar and usage • correct spelling • correct punctuation • correct capitalization	• few errors of grammar and usage • mostly correct spelling, punctuation, and capitalization	• errors in grammar, usage, and spelling sometimes make understanding difficult • some errors in punctuation and capitalization	• frequent errors in grammar, usage, spelling, capitalization, and punctuation make understanding difficult or impossible

Rubric for Expressive/Descriptive Writing

	4 Excellent	3 Very Good	2 Satisfactory	1 Needs Improvement
Content Quality and Idea Development	• "paints a picture" for the reader • well-focused on the topic • clear ideas are well-supported with interesting and vivid details	• creates some clear images for the reader • focused on the topic • ideas are well-supported with details	• sometimes strays from topic • ideas are not well-developed • more details are needed	• poorly focused on the topic • ideas are unclear • few details are given
Voice	• voice is fitting for the topic and engaging • well-suited for audience and purpose	• voice is fairly clear and seems to fit the topic • suited for audience and purpose	• voice rarely comes through • not always suited for audience and purpose	• voice is weak or inappropriate • no sense of audience or purpose
Organization	• well focused on the topic • logical organization • excellent transitions • easy to follow	• generally focused on the topic • some lapses in organization • some transitions • usually easy to follow	• somewhat focused on the topic • poor organization • few transitions • difficult to follow	• not focused on the topic • no clear organization • no transitions • difficult to impossible to follow
Word Precision	• precise, vivid, and interesting word choices • wide variety of word choices	• fairly precise, interesting, and somewhat varied word choices • wording could be more specific	• vague, mundane word choices • wording is sometimes repetitive • more descriptive words are needed	• very limited word choices • wording is bland and not descriptive
Sentence Fluency	• uses complete sentences • varying sentence structures and lengths	• uses complete sentences • generally simple sentence structures	• occasional sentence fragment or run-on sentence • simple sentence structure is used repeatedly	• frequent use of sentence fragments or run-on sentences • sentences are difficult to understand
Mechanics	• proper grammar and usage • correct spelling • correct punctuation • correct capitalization	• few errors of grammar and usage • mostly correct spelling, punctuation, and capitalization	• errors in grammar, usage, and spelling sometimes make understanding difficult • some errors in punctuation and capitalization	• frequent errors in grammar, usage, spelling, capitalization, and punctuation make understanding difficult or impossible

Rubric for Expository Writing

	4 Excellent	3 Very Good	2 Satisfactory	1 Needs Improvement
Content Quality and Idea Development	• well-focused on the topic • clear ideas are well-supported with interesting details	• focused on the topic • ideas are well-supported with details	• sometimes strays from topic • ideas are not well-developed • more details are needed	• poorly focused on the topic • ideas are unclear • few details are given
Voice	• voice is strong and engaging • well-suited for audience and purpose	• voice is fairly strong • suited for audience and purpose	• voice rarely comes through • not always suited for audience and purpose	• voice is weak or inappropriate • no sense of audience or purpose
Organization	• well-focused on the topic • logical organization • excellent transitions • easy to follow	• generally focused on the topic • organization is mostly clear • some transitions • usually easy to follow	• somewhat focused on the topic • poor organization • few transitions • difficult to follow	• not focused on the topic • no clear organization • no transitions • difficult to impossible to follow
Word Precision	• precise, interesting word choices • wide variety of word choices	• fairly precise, interesting word choices • wording could be more specific	• vague, mundane word choices • wording is sometimes repetitive	• very limited word choices • wording is bland
Sentence Fluency	• strong topic sentence • varying sentence structures and lengths • uses complete sentences	• good topic sentence • generally simple sentence structures • uses complete sentences	• weak topic sentence • simple sentence structure is used repeatedly • occasional sentence fragment or run-on sentence	• no topic sentence • sentences are difficult to understand • frequent use of sentence fragments or run-on sentences
Mechanics	• proper grammar and usage • correct spelling • correct punctuation • correct capitalization	• few errors of grammar and usage • mostly correct spelling, punctuation, and capitalization	• errors in grammar, usage, and spelling sometimes make understanding difficult • some errors in punctuation and capitalization	• frequent errors in grammar, usage, spelling, capitalization, and punctuation make understanding difficult or impossible

Social Studies Plus!

Class Projects Rubric

Social Studies Plus! presents numerous projects, for both individual and group work, making the rubric for the elements of content and skill more general. Many of the students' products resulting from these projects may be assessed as well by placing some in student portfolios or displaying them in the classroom. The rubric below is a general guide for assessing the projects.

Individual/Collaborative Projects

Directions: Copy the rubric for either groups or individuals. Circle the appropriate number for individual and collaborative participation in the projects.

Skill/Performance	Excellent	Very Good	Satisfactory	Needs Improvement
1. Collaborative reading/ understand task	4	3	2	1
2. Group listens to group leader	4	3	2	1
3. Group members listen to one another	4	3	2	1
4. Group understands cross-curricular skills needed	4	3	2	1
5. Group designs and constructs project in organized way	4	3	2	1
6. Individual uses right skills for environmental and historical research	4	3	2	1
7. Individual plans and executes art/craft project	4	3	2	1
8. Individual uses prior knowledge to complete task	4	3	2	1
9. Individual uses skill strategies, such as comparison, analysis, outlining, and map reading to complete task	4	3	2	1
10. Individual shows ability to reflect on what is the topic and what is important	4	3	2	1

Drama Rubric

Directions: Make a form for each student. Circle the appropriate number for each individual's participation in the play or scenario.

Student Name: _____

Skill/Performance	Excellent	Very Good	Satisfactory	Needs Improvement
1. Understands task	4	3	2	1
2. Plans own part	4	3	2	1
3. Understands the movement in front of group; maintains eye contact	4	3	2	1
4. Researched and practiced part	4	3	2	1
5. Willing to improvise in context	4	3	2	1
6. Projection and diction	4	3	2	1
7. Concentration and poise in acting	4	3	2	1
8. Language clear and delivered with enthusiasm	4	3	2	1
9. Understood content correctly	4	3	2	1
10. Delivered in believable way	4	3	2	1

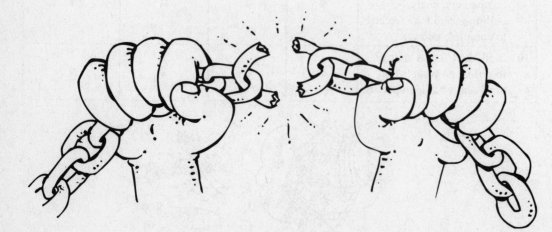

Glossary of Theater Terms

backdrop: a painting that shows the setting for a play; it hangs at the back of the stage, and scenes are played in front of it

blocking: setting the actors' positions and moves during rehearsal

center stage: in the middle of the stage

cue: a signal (a word, phrase, sound, or other action) to an actor or actors to enter, exit, or to begin a speech or action

downstage: the part of the stage that is nearest the audience

enter: to come onto the stage from the wings

exit: to leave the stage

Improv Directions: instructions for actors about moments when they must make up lines or actions

improvise: when actors make up material on the spot or in rehearsal

mime: a form of acting in which actions are used without words

monologue: a speech by one person

pantomime: the silent telling of a story through gestures, body movements, and facial expressions

pre-set: the set-up of the stage that is in place as the play begins

prologue: a short scene that comes before the main body of a play and introduces the theme

prop: any item needed by actors that they can carry on and off stage

ritual: a set of actions with special significance for the community, performed in a formal, stylized way

role-play: to improvise a character in a given situation

scene titles: signs written in large letters for the audience to read, announcing the titles of scenes

script: the written text of a play

scripted: written down, when all the lines are on the page

setting: when and where the action of a play occurs

stage directions: directions to the actors, usually in parentheses

stage right: the right-hand side from the actor's point of view, onstage, facing the audience

stage left: the left-hand side from the actor's point of view, onstage, facing the audience

tableau vivant or tableau: literally, a living picture; a scene where actors freeze to form a picture

unscripted: parts of a play that are not written down, where the actor(s) must improvise

upstage: relating to the rear of the stage

Teacher Planner

Long-Term Project pages 4–5	Materials	🕐	Lesson Link
A Quilting Party Students create a class quilt showing something special about our country.			Lessons 1–3
Week 1 👤👤👤 **group** Students brainstorm scenes from U.S. history that could be featured in their quilt square.	paper, pencils	1 session 20–30 min.	
Weeks 2 & 3 👤 **individual** Students create their quilt squares.	paper, old magazines, construction paper, art supplies	1 session 30–60 min.	
Week 4 👤👤👤 **group** Students decide how to arrange their squares to form a square or rectangular quilt section.	students' quilt squares, scissors, tape	1 session 30 min.	
Week 5 👤👤👤 **whole class** Students explain the special meaning of their quilt squares.	students' quilts	1 session 30–40 min.	
Unit Drama pages 6–11			
Play: America the Beautiful 👤👤👤 **group** Students perform a play about the meaning of the patriotic song "America the Beautiful."	none	1 session 40 min.	Lessons 1–3
Play: America 👤👤👤 **group** Students perform a play about the meaning of the patriotic song "America."	none	1 session 40 min.	Lessons 1–3
Play: This Land is Your Land 👤👤👤 **group** Students perform a play about the meaning of the patriotic song "This Land Is Your Land."	none	1 session 40 min.	Lessons 1–3
Chapter 1 Short-Term Projects pages 12–13			
Regional Tours 👤👤👤 **group** Students become regional tour guides for a day.	note paper or index cards, pencils	1 session 30 min.	Lesson 1
Post It 👤 **individual** Students create posters showing things in their region and a few words of text as captions.	paper or oaktag, crayons, markers, paints and brushes	1 session 20 min.	Lesson 1
Variety Show 👤👤 **partners** Students make landforms found in the country out of clay.	cardboard, clay	1 session 20 min.	Lesson 1
How Far from the Equator? 👤👤👤 **group** Students measure the distance from the equator to their region.	atlas, chart paper	1 session 20 min.	Lesson 2
Go with the Flow 👤👤 **partners** Students make flow charts showing how they think familiar objects got from raw materials to their present form.	paper, pencils, crayons, markers	1 session 20 min.	Lesson 2

Social Studies Plus!

Chapter **1** **Writing Projects** pages 14–15	Materials	🕐	**Lesson Link**
Landform Life 🚶 **individual** Students describe a landform for someone who has never seen it.	paper, pencils	1 session 20 min.	Lesson 1
Compare and Contrast Regions 🚶 **individual** Students write compositions comparing two different regions of the country.	paper, pencils	1 session 25 min.	Lessons 1–3
Pack Your Bags 🚶 **individual** Students make lists of the things they would need to pack for a trip to a particular region of the country.	paper, pencils	1 session 20 min.	Lesson 2
Conservation Editorial 🚶 **individual** Students summarize their views on why conservation is important.	paper, pencils	1 session 30 min.	Lesson 3

Chapter **1** **Citizenship Project** page 16			
Honesty 🚶🚶🚶 **whole class** Students describe honest ways of reacting to different situations.	BLM p. 17, paper, pencils	1 session 45 min.	Lessons 1–3

Chapter **2** **Short-Term Projects** pages 18–19			
From Start to Finish 🚶🚶🚶 **group** Students create maps showing where early explorers set out from and where they landed in North America.	world outline maps, crayons or markers, string, tape	1 session 20 min.	Lesson 1
"Go West!" Time Line 🚶🚶 **partners** Students show westward expansion on a time line.	paper, pencils, crayons or markers	1 session 20 min.	Lesson 1
"Government in Action" Mobile 🚶🚶 **partners** Students make mobiles representing the three branches of government.	oaktag, scissors, hole punches, string, wire hangers	1 session 20 min.	Lesson 2
Do You Have the Time? 🚶🚶 **partners** Students draw a series of four clocks and label the clocks by time zone, showing what time it is in each zone.	large sheets of paper or oaktag, crayons or markers	1 session 20 min.	Lesson 3
They Represent Us 🚶🚶🚶 **group** Students participate in a mock election.	paper, pencils	1 session 20 min.	Lesson 3

Chapter **2** **Writing Projects** pages 20–21			
Explorers' Letters 🚶 **individual** Students write letters to their families from aboard one of Columbus's ships.	paper, pencils	1 session 20 min.	Lesson 1
A Personal Bill of Rights 🚶 **individual** Students think about what sort of Bill of Rights they would write for themselves.	paper, pencils	1 session 20 min.	Lesson 3
Rights Diary 🚶 **individual** Students write diary entries explaining how citizens have recently made use of the freedoms granted by the Bill of Rights.	paper, pencils	1 session 25 min.	Lesson 3
Laws and Responsibilities 🚶 **individual** Students write paragraphs explaining the difference between laws and responsibilities.	paper, pencils	1 session 25 min.	Lesson 3

Chapter 2 Citizenship Project page 22	Materials	🕐	Lesson Link
Responsibility 🚶🚶🚶 whole class Students brainstorm responsibilities that different people have and what they have to do in order to fulfill them.	BLM p. 23, paper, pencils	1 session 45 min.	Lessons 1–3
Chapter 3 Short-Term Projects pages 24–25			
Wants and Needs Chart 🚶🚶🚶 group Students make charts listing their wants and needs, and then draw conclusions about the kinds of things they have listed.	markers, chart paper	1 session 20 min.	Lesson 1
Technology Wish List 🚶🚶 partners Students create "wish lists" of new technologies for practical problems that have yet to be solved.	paper, pencils	1 session 20 min.	Lesson 1
Funny Money 🚶🚶🚶 group Students design currency for their school.	paper, ruler, scissors, crayons or markers, clay	1 session 20 min.	Lesson 2
Let's Do Business 🚶🚶🚶 group Students plan their own businesses.	paper, pencils	1 session 30 min.	Lesson 2
Product Mobile 🚶🚶 partners Students create product mobiles out of pictures of products they use.	oaktag, crayons or markers, scissors, tape, string, hangers	1 session 20 min.	Lesson 3
Chapter 3 Writing Projects pages 26–27			
Country Mouse, City Mouse 🚶 individual Students compare and contrast living in a city and working in a factory with living and working on a farm.	paper, pencils	1 session 25 min.	Lesson 1
Making Choices 🚶 individual Students write diary entries describing their experience paying an opportunity cost.	paper, pencils	1 session 20 min.	Lesson 2
Persuasive Posters 🚶 individual Students write advertisements to persuade people in the community to buy their services.	paper, pencils, crayons or markers	1 session 25 min.	Lesson 2
Speedy Delivery: The U.S. Postal Service 🚶 individual Students write about how they think the postal system works.	paper, pencils	1 session 20 min.	Lesson 2
Happy Belated Birthday 🚶 individual Students write e-mail birthday cards to favorite family members or good friends.	paper, pencils	1 session 20 min.	Lesson 3
Chapter 3 Citizenship Project page 28			
Respect 🚶🚶🚶 whole class Students brainstorm ways people can respect each other's rights in different situations.	BLM p. 29, paper, pencils	1 session 40 min.	Lessons 1–3

NOTES

Long-Term Project

A Quilting Party

You're the host of a class quilting party! A "This Land Is Your Land" quilt comes together as each student contributes a square that shows something special about our country.

Brainstorm Subjects for Quilt Squares

Week 1

👫👫 group   🕐 20–30 minutes

Materials: paper, pencils

Encourage your class to talk about quilts, what they look like, how they are used, and how they are made. Then invite students to a quilting party.

• Make sure students know that in Colonial times quilting parties were a regular feature of social life. Each person made a square, and then the group sewed the squares together to make a quilt. Tell students that each of them will make a square for a This Land Is Your Land paper quilt about living in the United States.

• Lead the class in brainstorming what could be shown on the squares, (mountains, trees, a quote from the Constitution, a scene from U.S. history, a famous American, or an example of U.S. currency).

• Divide the class into groups to brainstorm further.

Make the Quilt Squares

Weeks 2 & 3

🧍 individual   🕐 30–60 minutes

Materials: white or colored paper, rulers, scissors, crayons or markers, construction paper, old magazines, paste

Establish a standard size for the squares so that they can be put together easily. Have each student cut a sheet of paper to the correct size. Tell students to be sure to leave a margin of about one inch around their squares for taping the quilt together. Students can create their squares by drawing their own pictures or by pasting cutout shapes from construction paper or photos from old magazines.

Put It All Together

Week 4

Materials: students' quilt squares, scissors, plain or colored masking tape

Have students meet in their groups again to decide how to arrange their squares to form a square or rectangular quilt section. Show the students how to tape the squares together with masking tape. (Masking tape is recommended because it can be easily removed and reapplied if children make a mistake.) When the groups have taped their sections together, clear an area big enough to lay all the sections down, or tack them to a bulletin board so that they fit together. Tape the sections together to complete the This Land Is Your Land quilt. Display the quilt prominently in the classroom.

"We the People of the United States"

Quilt Talk

Week 5

Materials: the quilt

Give each child time to point to his or her square and briefly explain its special meaning to the class. Students may talk about why they chose their particular subjects, what their subjects represent, and how their subjects relate to life in the United States. The class could celebrate the completion of their quilt by singing the first verse of the song "This Land Is Your Land."

America the Beautiful

Most of us know at least a few patriotic songs such as "America the Beautiful." But have we ever stopped to think about what the words to these songs really mean?

The Parts: (5 players)
- Student 1
- Student 2
- Student 3
- Student 4
- Student 5

Director's Notes: With your group, go over the song "America the Beautiful" to make sure students know the words. Some players will improvise, or make up, their lines. Discuss what players might say about the meaning of each line in the song. Tell players to watch for stage directions in the play. They are shown in parentheses.

(All sing the first verse of "America the Beautiful" together.)

America the Beautiful

Oh beautiful for spacious skies
For amber waves of grain
For purple mountains' majesty
Above the fruited plain
America! America!
God shed his grace on thee.
And crown thy good
With brotherhood
From sea to shining sea.

Student 1:   I wonder what the words to that song really mean?

Student 2:   Yeah, like what are "spacious skies"?

Student 3:   *(Improv Directions: Improvises what "spacious skies" may mean.)*

Student 4:   What about "amber waves of grain"? What's *amber*, anyway?

Student 5:   *Amber* is a light brownish-yellow color. But what are waves of grain? I thought waves were in the ocean.

© Scott Foresman 4

*(**Improv Directions:** Other students improvise discussion about the meaning of "amber waves of grain.")*

Student 1: Okay. So far, so good. But what about "purple mountains' majesty"? Did you ever see a purple mountain? And what about "majesty"? "Your Majesty" is something you call a king or queen.

Student 2: When the sun sets behind the mountains, it makes the mountains look purple sometimes. And *majesty* probably means the mountains are as great as kings or queens.

Student 3: I bet no one gets this one: "Above the fruited plain."

Student 4: We learned that a plain is a flat piece of land.

Student 5: *(**Improv Directions:** Improvises what he or she thinks a fruited plain is.)*

Student 1: I know what "God shed his grace on thee" means. It means "God bless America!" And "crown thy good with brotherhood" means . . . *(**Improv Directions:** Continues to improvise.)*

Student 2: And "from sea to shining sea" means from the Atlantic to the Pacific!

Student 1: I think I finally get it.

(All sing "America the Beautiful" again, but with more feeling.)

America

Although the title of this song is "America," lots of people call it by its first line, "My country 'tis of thee." Do you know what that line means? If not, you're about to find out.

The Parts: (5 players)
- Student 1
- Student 2
- Student 3
- Student 4
- Student 5

Director's Notes: With your group, go over the song "America" to make sure students know the words. Some players will improvise, or make up, their lines. Discuss what players might say about the meaning of each line in the song.

Tell players to watch for stage directions in parentheses.

(All sing the first verse of the song "America" together. They are a group of students marching in a parade on a national holiday.)

America

My country 'tis of thee,
Sweet land of liberty,
Of thee I sing.
Land where my fathers died,
Land of the pilgrims' pride,
From every mountainside—
Let freedom ring.

Student 1: I love marching in parades.

Student 2: Me too, but I don't like that song because I don't know what it means.

Student 3: Neither do I. I don't even understand how it starts. What does "'tis of thee" mean?

*(**Improv Directions:** Other students improvise their ideas about the meaning of the beginning of the song: "My country 'tis of thee, sweet land of liberty, of thee I sing.")*

Social Studies Plus!

Student 4: Okay, we figured that out. Why do the words say "land where my fathers died"? It sounds so depressing!

*(**Improv Directions:** Other students improvise discussion about "land where my fathers died.")*

Student 5: I think we're on a roll. What about "land of the pilgrims' pride"?

*(**Improv Directions:** Other students improvise discussion about "land of the pilgrims' pride.")*

Student 1: We're almost at the end. How about, "from every mountainside, let freedom ring"?

Student 2: Well, if you turn the words around, it's "let freedom ring from every mountainside."

*(**Improv Directions:** Other students improvise discussion of "from every mountainside, let freedom ring.")*

Student 3: So what does the whole song mean?

*(**Improv Directions:** All students improvise a summary of the meaning of the entire song.)*

This Land Is Your Land

"This land is your land, this land is my land."
Whose land is it, anyway? This folksong is fun to sing . . .
and its words carry a very important message.

The Parts: (6 players)
- Student 1
- Student 2
- Student 3
- Student 4
- Student 5
- Guitar Player (an older person holding a guitar)

Director's Notes: With your group, go over the song "This Land Is Your Land" to make sure students know the words. Some players will improvise, or make up, their lines. With your group, brainstorm what players might say about the meaning of each line in the song. Tell your players to watch for stage directions that are shown in parentheses. If you don't have a guitar handy, you can make a cutout guitar or the Guitar Player can pretend.

Theater Talk

prop: an object players use on a stage

(All sing the first verse of the song "This Land Is Your Land" together. They are a group of students sitting around a campfire.)

This Land Is Your Land
Words and Music by Woody Guthrie ©

This land is your land,
This land is my land
From California
To the New York Island;
From the redwood forests
To the Gulf Stream waters;
This land was made for you and me.

© Scott Foresman 4

Student 1:	Camping is really fun.
Student 2:	The best part is singing songs around the campfire.
Guitar Player:	Did you know that the song we just sang was written by a famous folksong writer and singer named Woody Guthrie? What do you think his words mean?
Student 3:	I wonder why it starts out "This land is *your* land, this land is *my* land." Whose land *is* it—yours or mine?
Student 4:	I think he means that it belongs to everyone. And I think that's really true!
Guitar Player:	What about the words "from California to the New York Island" and "from the redwood forests to the Gulf Stream waters?"
Student 5:	When the song says "the New York Island," it probably means Manhattan Island where New York City is.
Student 1:	The Gulf Stream waters must mean the Gulf of Mexico. That's in between Texas and Florida.
Student 2:	And the redwood forests are in northern California.
	(Improv Directions: Other students improvise discussion about the meaning of "from California to the New York Island, from the redwood forests to the Gulf Stream waters.")
Student 3:	It's true. This country sure is big.
Student 4:	And it has lots of different kinds of places.
Student 5:	I guess we all know what "this land was made for you and me" means.
Guitar Player:	So what important message did Woody Guthrie want to send to all of us?
	(Improv Directions: All students improvise about the meaning of the entire song.)

Short-Term Projects

**Do your students know their way around the United States—
its varied places and abundant resources? Here are some projects
that let students show what they know!**

Regional Tours

👫 group   🕐 30 minutes

Materials: note paper or index cards, pencils

Students showcase their knowledge of different regions in the United States as they become regional tour guides for a day.

1. Start out by forming groups of five students or less. Then, on separate sheets of paper or index cards, have a student write the name of each of the five regions of the United States.

2. The group then chooses a dealer who shuffles the cards and deals one card to each group member, face down.

3. In turn, each student acts as a tour guide for his or her region by telling a few facts about the region, such as its resources, climate, or states located there. The other students should be encouraged to take notes and to ask questions of their tour guide.

Post It

🧍 individual   🕐 20 minutes

Materials: large sheets of paper or oaktag, crayons, markers, paints, brushes

A travel poster shows the beautiful and interesting aspects of a place so that people who see the poster will want to visit there. Invite students to pick out one or more things in their own region that people from other places would like to see. Have them create posters showing the things they've chosen and a few words of text such as "Come out west—it's wild!" Display the posters on a bulletin board headed "Come to (the name of your region)."

Variety Show

👥 partners 🕐 20 minutes

Materials: sheets of cardboard, modeling clay

Invite students to show the variety of landforms in our country by making models of the landforms they've learned about, for example, mountains, plains, deserts, canyons, plateaus, or rolling hills. Have students make their landforms out of modeling clay on a cardboard base. Display their finished products in a "landforms museum" in the classroom.

How Far from the Equator?

👥 group 🕐 20 minutes

Materials: atlas, chart paper

The distance of an area from the equator is an important influence on the area's climate. Invite small groups of students to make charts that prove this point.

1. Have each group choose two cities in the United States that have different climates from your area. (For example, if you are in San Francisco, students might choose Portland, Maine, and Miami Beach, Florida.)

2. Have them use an atlas to measure the approximate distance in miles from the equator to your area and the two other cities.

3. Invite students to make charts showing the distances.

4. Groups can meet together to compare their charts and draw a conclusion about their results—places nearer the equator are usually warmer than places farther away from the equator.

> **Remember! Keep working on that Long-Term Project.**

Go with the Flow

👥 partners 🕐 20 minutes

Materials: paper, pencils, crayons, markers

Encourage students to think about how their clothing and school supplies go from raw materials to the objects they wear and use. For example, a wool sweater starts with a sheep that gets a "haircut." The wool is spun into yarn and is knitted by hand or machine into something to keep us warm. Have partners make simple flow charts that show in words or pictures how they think familiar objects got from raw materials to their present forms. Display the charts on a Go with the Flow bulletin board.

Writing Projects

Harness your students' powers of imagination and creativity
with these writing activities to deepen their understanding
of the regions and resources of the United States.

Landform Life

Invite students to choose one (or more) of the landforms introduced in this chapter—for example, mountains, plains, deserts, plateaus, or rolling hills. Ask students to imagine they live on or near that landform. Then encourage students to think about how they would describe their personal relation to the landform to someone who has never seen it. For example, students could describe the heat of a desert or the endless skies of the plains. They could write about the landform's plant and animal life or about recreational or other activities that may take place there. Encourage students to use descriptive language. They might accompany their paragraphs with drawings or diagrams.

Pack Your Bags

Invite students to choose particular places that they would like to visit in the five regions of the United States. What would they pack if they were going to visit those places? Have each student make a packing list including clothing and other items appropriate for the regions, such as a snowboard for visiting the Northeast or the West, swim fins and a snorkel for visiting the Southeast, hiking boots for the Southwest, and so on. In making their lists, students should consider both the climates and landforms of the regions they will visit. Encourage students to use their own judgment to decide whether or not they need to specify a season for their imaginary trips. They should also decide for themselves how they will organize their lists by category. They might use two headings—Clothing and Equipment. Or they might separate articles of clothing into different categories, such as indoor clothing and outdoor clothing.

© Scott Foresman 4

Compare and Contrast Regions

Throughout this chapter, students have been exploring the five regions of the United States and finding that each one has its own particular character. A combination of climate, landforms, and resources makes each region unique. Some characteristics can be found in more than one region, however. Invite students to choose two regions that interest them and write compositions of one or more paragraphs comparing and contrasting those regions.

• Before students write, they should think about how they will organize their compositions. They might write one paragraph about similarities and a second paragraph about differences. Or they might write a paragraph showing similarities and differences in climate, another showing similarities and differences in landforms, and another showing similarities and differences in natural resources.

• They may want to end their composition with a summary of why they may prefer one region to the other.

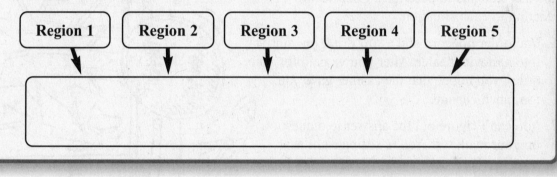

Conservation Editorial

Students learn from many different sources that conservation is important to our environment. They read and hear that we shouldn't waste resources, that we should recycle, and that we should try to prevent pollution of land, water, and air.

• Invite students to think about why conservation is important and to summarize their views in newspaper editorials. You may help students by generating a list of familiar conservation methods on the chalkboard that students may choose to discuss in their editorials.

• Remind students that the purpose of an editorial is to persuade readers to agree with the writer's opinions. Therefore, they should be sure to give strong reasons and use logical arguments to prove the points they wish to make.

Citizenship

Honesty

**Everyone learns that it's good to be honest.
But honesty can mean more than speaking the truth.
Most often actions speak louder than words.**

The first thing we think of when we think of honesty is telling the truth when we are asked a question. ("Did you eat all those cookies?" "Yes, I did.") Suggest to students that sometimes honesty poses even more difficult problems than owning up to doing something you weren't supposed to do. Sometimes being honest involves actions as well as or instead of words.

Present the following three situations to the class, and ask students to describe an honest way of reacting to each situation:

1. You order popcorn and a soft drink on your way into a movie theater. After you've paid for your order, you notice that the cashier gave you too much change.

2. You can't figure out the answer to a question on your math test. You're sitting right near your teacher's desk, and you notice that he has accidentally left his copy of the answers where you can see it. No one would ever find out if you looked.

3. You and your friends are playing ball in a field near an apartment building. Someone misses a catch and the ball smashes a window in an apartment. No one is home, so no one saw the window get broken.

Invite students to discuss the honest way to approach each situation. Then talk about the reasons why it's important to be honest. What are the advantages of being honest even when a person might seem to benefit from acting dishonestly?

Have students complete the blackline master on page 17 by writing a fable that teaches the lesson Honesty Is the Best Policy. Remind students that a fable is a very short story, usually with talking animal characters, that teaches a lesson or ends with a *moral*. As an example, you might tell a brief version of one of Aesop's fables, such as "The Tortoise and the Hare."

© Scott Foresman 4

A Fable About Honesty

On the lines, write your own fable. Use animal characters who can talk. Your fable should teach the lesson Honesty Is the Best Policy. Write the lesson at the end of the fable.

Chapter 2 — Short-Term Projects

From unexplored land to vibrant democracy, the United States
has come a long way. With these hands-on projects, students learn what makes
"the land of the free and the home of the brave" so great.

From Start to Finish

👤👤 group   🕐 20 minutes

Materials: world outline maps, crayons or markers, yarn or string, tape

During the fifteenth and sixteenth centuries, explorers came from Europe to a world that
was new to them. Part of that world would someday become the United States. Invite
students to create maps that show where these explorers set out from and where they
landed in North America.

1. Divide the class into small groups, and give each group an outline map of the world.

2. Have each group choose three explorers introduced in the chapter. Encourage groups to
   choose different explorers so as many as possible will be represented.

3. Students will show on their maps where each explorer began and ended his
   journey. They may use markers or crayons, or they may tape lengths of
   string or yarn to the map. Each "route" should be labeled with the
   explorer's name.

4. Display the maps on a bulletin board with the
   heading Where Did They Come From? Where
   Did They Go?

"Go West!" Time Line

👤 partners   🕐 20 minutes

Materials: paper, pencils, crayons or markers

The original United States of America consisted of thirteen colonies huddled along the
Atlantic coast of North America. Less than a hundred years after declaring its independence,
the new nation stretched approximately three thousand miles all the way to the Pacific Ocean.

Invite students to show westward expansion on a time line. The following are some
landmark dates they should include: Mississippi River reached by 1783; Rocky Mountains
reached by 1803; Texas added 1845; Oregon Territory added in 1846; land in Southwest
purchased from Mexico in 1848; Pacific Ocean reached by 1853.

"Government in Action" Mobile

partners · **20 minutes**

Materials: oaktag, scissors, hole punches, string, wire hangers

The framers of the Constitution created a government divided into three branches. Our government today is organized the same way today. Invite students to make mobiles that represent that structure. Their mobiles should reflect the following: the three main branches of the U.S. government (executive, legislative, judicial); the president and vice president under the executive branch; the House of Representatives and Senate under the legislative branch; and the Supreme Court and federal courts under the judicial branch.

Do You Have the Time?

partners · **20 minutes**

Materials: large sheets of paper or oaktag, crayons or markers

It may be 9:00 A.M. in your time zone, but some people in the country may just be getting up and others may be having lunch. Invite students to draw a series of four clocks—one for each time zone in the continental United States. Have them label the clocks by time zone and show what time it is in each zone when it is 9:00 A.M. where you live.

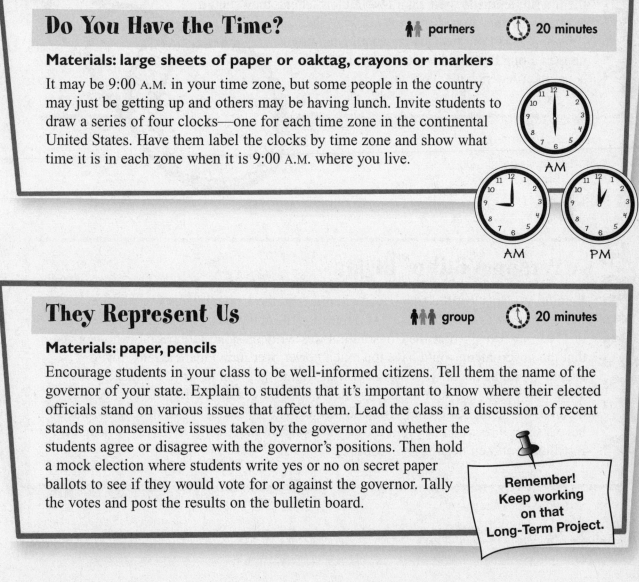

AM

AM   PM

They Represent Us

group · **20 minutes**

Materials: paper, pencils

Encourage students in your class to be well-informed citizens. Tell them the name of the governor of your state. Explain to students that it's important to know where their elected officials stand on various issues that affect them. Lead the class in a discussion of recent stands on nonsensitive issues taken by the governor and whether the students agree or disagree with the governor's positions. Then hold a mock election where students write yes or no on secret paper ballots to see if they would vote for or against the governor. Tally the votes and post the results on the bulletin board.

Remember! Keep working on that Long-Term Project.

Writing Projects

Students get personal as they write about what they've learned in this chapter as it applies to their everyday lives.

Explorers' Letters

It's not hard to imagine the lure of adventure that called to many of the young men who joined Columbus on his voyages. If students think about their own families, they'll be able to consider the possibility that many of those young men's families were not so pleased to see their sons go off to face unknown dangers. Invite your students to suppose they are aboard one of Columbus's ships and have them write letters to their families. In their letters, they should explain why they joined the voyage, what they hope to find, and what their worries are about what might happen along the way. Encourage students to share their letters with classmates.

A Personal Bill of Rights

Remind students that the first ten amendments to the United States Constitution are what we know as the Bill of Rights. The Bill of Rights was added to the Constitution in 1791—two years after the Constitution was written—to assure people who worried that the government would have too much power over individual citizens. Invite students to think about what sort of Bill of Rights they would write for themselves. Would they want the right to stay up late? Would they want the right to change the menu in the school cafeteria? Ask students to write a personal "Bill of Rights." Then have a short discussion to explore what is important in students' lives and whether the fulfillment of their desires is reasonable.

Social Studies Plus!

Rights Diary

The Bill of Rights was written long ago, but it still protects and benefits United States citizens—right here and now. Encourage your students to think about how some of the freedoms granted to us by the Bill of Rights affect them personally in their everyday lives. Have them write diary entries explaining how they recently made use of freedom of speech, freedom of religion, or freedom of the press (the right to express one's ideas in writing).

Laws and Responsibilities

We live in a democracy, and we value our many freedoms. But freedom doesn't mean we can do whatever we want. We live by laws, which we must obey. We also have responsibilities—things we should do to be good citizens, but that we are not *required* to do by law. For example, we must pay taxes—that's the law. Citizens who are eighteen years of age or more have the right to vote, but they are not required to do so. Exercising one's right to vote is a responsibility—not a law. Share these examples with your class, and encourage them to think about the differences between laws and responsibilities. Invite them to write well-organized paragraphs explaining those differences.

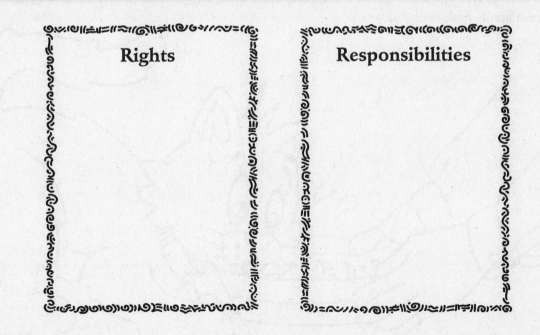

Rights

Responsibilities

Citizenship

Responsibility

Responsibility is a word children hear often. They have chores and they have homework. Have students play the Responsibility Game to learn more about this big word.

Ask your students what they think of when they think of the word *responsibility*. In discussion, bring out that when we talk about being responsible, we usually mean being responsible *for* something or someone. In other words, being responsible means taking care of something or someone. It means keeping promises and doing what we've agreed to do or what we're supposed to do.

• Invite students to brainstorm responsibilities that different people have and what they have to do in order to fulfill them. List students' ideas on the chalkboard. As the list of ideas grows, categorize them under headings such as Parents, Teachers, Students, Friends, Sons and Daughters, Pet Owners, Bike Riders, Newspaper Reporters, Store Owners, and so on.

• Next, discuss why it's important to be a responsible person. How does being a responsible person make you feel about yourself? How much responsibility should a fourth grader have?

• Distribute copies of the blackline master on page 23 and have students work in pairs or small groups to create game cards. Instruct them to fill in the blanks to complete the sentences: "Be a responsible _____ (e.g., student, pet owner)." Then have them cut the cards apart with scissors.

• Students can play the Responsibility Game by picking a card and naming something the person on the card could do to show that he or she is responsible. The cards can be reused until each player has had a turn. (If someone can't think of a responsibility for that card, have other students make suggestions.)

The Responsibility Game

Students are to fill in the blanks to complete each sentence, then cut the cards apart. To play the Responsibility Game, students pick a card and name a responsibility of the person on that card. If a student can't think of a responsibility, the other players are responsible for helping!

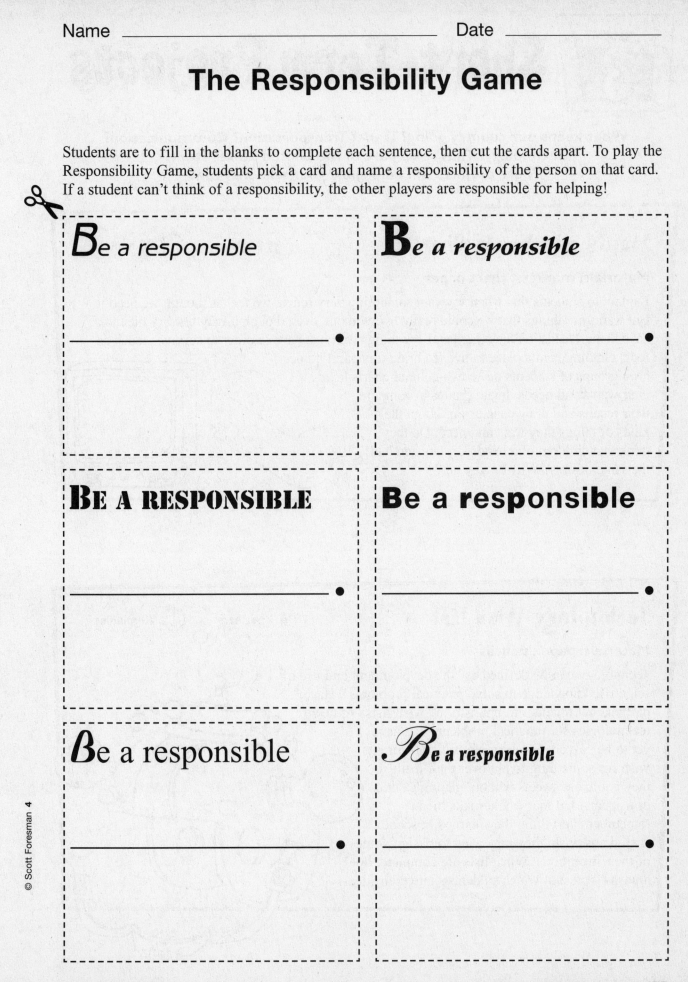

*B*e a responsible

_____ •

Be a responsible

_____ •

BE A RESPONSIBLE

_____ •

Be a responsible

_____ •

*B*e a responsible

_____ •

Be a responsible

_____ •

Short-Term Projects

What keeps our country going? Trade? Transportation? Communication?
Technology? They're *all* part of the United States story.
These projects will help show your students why.

Wants and Needs Chart

👫👤 group   🕐 20 minutes

Materials: markers, chart paper

Explain to students that when we want something very much, we feel as though we need it. But wants are things that we could really live without, even though it may be very nice to have them. Needs, on the other hand, are things we must have in order to survive—such as food, clothing, and a place to live. To bring this point home, have groups of students make two-column charts listing their wants and needs. Invite groups to compare their results and draw conclusions about the kinds of things they want and need. Do they think that children of a hundred years ago had the same desires? Why or why not?

Technology Wish List

👤👤 partners   🕐 20 minutes

Materials: paper, pencils

Technology can be defined as "the development and use of scientific knowledge to solve practical problems." Have partners get together to brainstorm "wish lists" of new technologies for practical problems that have yet to be solved. For example, students might wish for something to put over their teeth so they could eat sweets without getting cavities or a special hat that would make them remember everything they learned in school. If students wish, they may want to design some of their inventions. When lists are complete, hold a wish-list fest at which students share their ideas.

© Scott Foresman 4

Funny Money

👥 group   🕐 20 minutes

Materials: paper, ruler, scissors, crayons or markers, clay

What if your school had its own currency? Invite small groups of students to design money for your school. They should decide whether to use bills, coins, or both, what the basic denomination will be, and what the coins and/or bills will be called. To get design ideas, let students look at examples of U.S. coins and bills. What pictures do they see? What words? Encourage students to use pictures and words on their own money that stand for something about their school, as U.S. currency uses pictures and words that stand for aspects of the United States. Students can cut bills out of paper and use clay for making coins. Create a "money museum" in the classroom to display the currency students have created.

> **Remember!**
> **Keep working**
> **on that**
> **Long-Term Project.**

Let's Do Business

👥 group   🕐 30 minutes

Materials: paper, pencils

Invite students to plan their own businesses. Have groups brainstorm what goods or services they could provide that people in your school or community might want to buy or use. How much will they charge their customers? How much will it cost them to run their business? How much profit do they plan to make? Students may plan business ventures such as making and selling cookies or crafts or providing services such as dog walking or baby-sitting. Set aside time for students to share their business plans.

Cookies by Carlos

Product Mobile

👤 partners   🕐 20 minutes

Materials: oaktag, crayons or markers, scissors, tape, string, wire hangers

Invite students to get together with partners and brainstorm manufactured products they use, such as video games, CD players, scooters, or running shoes. Have students work together to draw pictures of these products, cut them out, and make product mobiles. Students should label each product. Display the mobiles around the classroom.

© Scott Foresman 4

Writing Projects

**Making choices, earning money, starting a business—
the following writing activities can help students explore these issues.**

Making Choices

Students have learned that an "opportunity cost" is the thing you give up if you want two things but can afford only one. Most of us have had the experience of paying an opportunity cost. Invite students to discuss times when they had to pay such a cost. For example, they may have had to choose between two video games, or between a new bike and a computer. Then have them write diary entries describing their experiences. Would they make the same choices again? Why or why not? Let students know that their entries can be fictional—they don't have to write about experiences they've really had. When students share their entries, they can discuss whether they agree with each other's choices.

Persuasive Posters

Ask students to suppose that they are planning to make extra spending money by providing services that people in their community would be willing to pay for. With the class, brainstorm what some services might be: dog-walking, baby-sitting, washing cars, raking leaves, and so on. Then invite students to write advertisements to post in a local supermarket to persuade people in the community to buy their services. An ad should make people feel that they need the service and that the student who has posted the ad will do a better job than anyone else. Remind students to use strong persuasive language.

© Scott Foresman 4

Speedy Delivery: The U.S. Postal Service

Do your students fully understand what happens to a letter between the time the sender puts a stamp on the envelope and drops it in a mailbox and the time a mail carrier delivers it to the addressee? Have students write about how they think the system works. Remind students that in explaining a process they should be careful to use clear and correct sequencing. Students may share their thoughts with the class or research the U.S. Postal Service at a later time to see how close they came to the mark.

Happy Belated Birthday

Ask students to suppose that they have forgotten to send a birthday card to a friend or relative. They're in big trouble now! But not really—because today's technology makes instant communication possible. Invite students to write e-mail birthday cards to favorite family members or good friends. Encourage them to make their greetings creative or unique. Remind students to save their greetings for a time when they might really send them to those special people.

Country Mouse, City Mouse

Present students with the following scenario: You are living back at the beginning of the twentieth century—about a hundred years ago. You have been working on a farm, but then you move to a big city to get a better job in a factory. You are writing a letter to a friend or relative describing your new life. Have students write letters describing their new lives. Students should compare and contrast living in a city and working in a factory with living and working on a farm. Each writer can end by telling whether he or she thinks this new life is an improvement or not.

Citizenship

Respect

Respect. What is it? Maybe it's all summed up in the Golden Rule: Do unto others as you would have others do unto you. Or in simpler language, treat others the way you would like to be treated.

Children are taught that they should respect others. Discuss with the class what this means—to treat others thoughtfully, speak politely to them, and try not to hurt their feelings. In other words, respecting others means treating them the way you would like them to treat you. Then extend the discussion to include respecting the *rights* of others. Guide students to understand that everyone has rights, but sometimes people's rights get in each other's way. That's when respecting each other is most important.

Invite students to think of ways people can respect each other's rights in situations such as the following:

1. You and your friends are playing loud music on the radio. It's annoying your neighbor who is trying to concentrate on a book he is reading. You have a right to play music. After all, it's the middle of the afternoon—not late at night. But your neighbor has the right to read his book too.

2. The family that lives in the house next door paints their house bright purple with lime-green trim around the doors and windows. All the other people on the street say it makes the whole street look horrible. The family has a right to choose the color of their house, but the other families on the block have a right to live in a place that looks nice.

3. You are watching a movie in a movie theater. The people sitting next to you have brought their baby with them, and the baby keeps crying so you can't hear the movie. They have a right to take their baby with them, but you paid for your tickets and you have a right to hear the movie.

Invite students to role-play one or more of the situations you've presented or some that they think up themselves. Then have each use a copy of the blackline master on page 29 to describe a situation in which people have to compromise in order to respect each other's rights. Students should suggest a solution that would allow everyone's rights to be respected. Display students' writing on a bulletin board with the title Show Some Respect.

© Scott Foresman 4

Name _____ Date _____

Show Some Respect

Use this box to describe a situation in which two people are getting in the way of each other's rights.

Use this box to write a solution to the problem. How can the two people solve their problem so that everyone's rights will be respected?

Long-Term Project pages 32–33	Materials	⏱	Lesson Link
We the Students Students create their own class constitution.			Lessons 1–2
Week 1 🚹🚹🚹 whole class Students look over the United States Constitution in order to get a feeling for its parts.	copies of the Constitution, pencils, paper	1 session 30 min.	
Week 2 🚹🚹🚹 group Students think of three to five laws that will help everyone in the class get along.	pencils, paper	1 session 30–60 min.	
Week 3 🚹🚹🚹 whole class Students debate on any details with which groups or individuals disagree.	chalkboard, students' notes from Week 2	1 session 20–30 min.	
Week 4 🚹🚹🚹 whole class Students hold a nominating session for class officers.	none	1 session 30–60 min.	
Weeks 5 & 6 🚹🚹🚹 whole class Students hold an election and post their constitution.	chart paper or craft paper, marker	1 session 20–40 min.	

Unit Drama pages 34–39

Play: Winter Wonderland 🚹🚹🚹 group Students perform a play about the Northeast region of the United States.	props and costumes (optional)	1 session 40 min.	Lesson 1
Play: Hello, Sweet Spring! 🚹🚹🚹 group Students perform a play about what happens during the spring season.	props and costumes (optional)	1 session 40 min.	Lesson 1
Play: Summer and Fall 🚹🚹🚹 group Students perform a play about summer and autumn in the Northeast.	props and costumes (optional)	1 session 40 min.	Lessons 1–3
Scenarios: Explore the Northeast 🚹🚹🚹 group Students role-play skits about the places of the varied Northeast.	props (optional)	7 sessions 25 min. each	

Chapter 4 Short-Term Projects pages 40–41

Make a Model 🚹🚹 partners Students create models of the different landforms they have studied in the chapter.	cardboard or oaktag, clay, paints and brushes	1 session 40 min.	Lesson 1
Power Flow 🚹 individual Students make flow charts showing how a hydropower plant produces electricity.	large sheets of paper, crayons or markers	1 session 20 min.	Lesson 1
Calling All Leaf Peepers! 🚹 individual Students create travel posters inviting people to come to the Northeast to see and share autumn in all its glory.	large sheets of paper or oaktag, crayons, markers, paints and brushes	1 session 20 min.	Lesson 1

Chapter **4** **Short-Term Projects** *continued*	**Materials**	🕐	**Lesson Link**
What Will You Have? 👪 group Students create their own menus for a seafood restaurant in the Chesapeake Bay area.	paper, pencils, crayons or markers	1 session 20 min.	Lesson 3
Give Me Your Tired 👪 group Students present "The New Colossus" by Emma Lazarus to their fellow classmates.	copies of "The New Colossus," by Emma Lazarus	1 session 45 min.	Lesson 3
Bay Watchers 👫 partners Students debate each side of an important environmental issue.	none	1 session 15 min.	Lesson 3

Chapter **4** **Writing Projects** pages 42–43			
Appalachian Poem 👤 individual Students write poems about their experiences on the Appalachian Trail.	paper, pencils	1 session 25 min.	Lesson 1
Pen Pal Letter 👤 individual Students describe autumn or winter in the Northeast to a pen pal.	paper, pencils	1 session 20 min.	Lesson 1
A Weekend Trip 👤 individual Students research a vacation spot they would like to visit in the Northeast and write schedules for a weekend trip.	paper, pencils	1 session 20 min.	Lesson 1
Is it a Berry? 👤 individual Students write their own definitions of a berry.	paper, pencils	1 session 20 min.	Lesson 2

Chapter **4** **Citizenship Project** page 44			
Caring 👪 whole class Students plan projects that show caring through action.	BLM p. 45, paper, pencils	1 session 45 min.	Lessons 1–3

Chapter **5** **Short-Term Projects** pages 46–47			
The Narragansett Way 👪 group Students make a list of the ways they can cooperate with each other.	paper, pencils	1 session 20 min.	Lesson 1
Wigwam Models 👫 partners Students create models of a wigwam.	pipe cleaners, tape, fabric or tissue paper, scissors	1 session 20 min.	Lesson 1
History Trail 👫 partners Students list sites and historical events that happened in the Northeast.	road maps of the Northeast, markers, pencils, paper	1 session 20 min.	Lessons 1–2
"Concord Hymn" 👪 whole class/individual 👤 Students read "Concord Hymn" and illustrate it.	chalkboard, paper, pencils, crayons	1 session 20 min.	Lesson 2
Help Wanted 👫 partners Students look over the "Help Wanted" section of the local newspaper and discuss jobs that interest them.	"Help Wanted" section of a local newspaper, art supplies	1 session 20 min.	Lesson 2

Chapter **5** Writing Projects pages 48–49	Materials	🕐	Lesson Link
Native American Place Names 👤 individual Students make up new names in English for places with which they are familiar.	paper, pencils	1 session 20 min	Lesson 1
Lecture Summary: The Iroquois Constitution 👤 individual Students write summaries of a lecture on the Iroquois government.	paper, pencils	1 session 30 min.	Lesson 1
Tale of Two Cities 👤 individual Students compare and contrast the Northeast's three biggest cities: New York, Boston, and Philadelphia.	paper, pencils	1 session 20 min.	Lesson 4
Immigrant's Journal 👤 individual Students write journal entries of an immigrant telling how they feel as they see the Statue of Liberty for the first time.	paper, pencils	1 session 20 min.	Lesson 4
Chapter **5** Citizenship Project page 50			
Respect 👤👤👤 whole class Students list ways of showing respect for others in a variety of situations.	BLM p. 51, paper, pencils	1 session 45 min.	Lessons 1–4

© Scott Foresman 4

Social Studies Plus!

NOTES

Long-Term Project

We the Students

The Northeast is our nation's birthplace—the region where our founders met to draft the Constitution. Your students can celebrate the Northeast by working cooperatively to create their own class constitution.

Introduce the U.S. Constitution

Week 1

👤👤👤 whole class   🕐 30 minutes

Materials: copies of the Constitution, pencils, paper

Distribute copies of the United States Constitution, and give students a chance to look them over. They should try to get a feeling of the Constitution as a whole and of its different parts—the preamble, the articles, and the amendments.

Lead students to see that the Constitution is really a set of rules that tells how our government works: how the president is elected and what the president's jobs are; how laws are made; and how people who commit crimes are tried and punished. Explain that the Bill of Rights protects the rights of people living in the United States. Encourage students to give their own ideas about the Constitution, its purpose, and its contents.

Brainstorm a Class Constitution

Week 2

👤👤 group   🕐 30–60 minutes

Materials: pencils, paper

Divide the class into groups, and have students talk about creating a constitution for the class. Before the groups meet, let students know that they cannot make *all* the rules for the class. Some rules have already been made by the school and the state in which you live. Tell them that you, the teacher, will have the right to veto any law that goes against school rules or that seems inappropriate.

Tell students they should concentrate on class officers and their jobs, how these officers should be nominated and elected, and what their terms of office will be. They should also think of three to five laws that will help everyone in the class get along. Finally, they should consider ways to amend the constitution, if necessary. Each group should appoint a note taker to write down the group's ideas.

© Scott Foresman 4

Hold a Meeting

👫👫 whole class   🕐 20–30 minutes

Materials: chalkboard, students' notes from Week 2

Hold a class meeting, during which groups can compare and contrast their ideas for the class constitution. Encourage debate on any details with which groups or individuals disagree. If students cannot come to unanimous agreements on any detail, hold a vote. Keep a record of ideas on which the majority of students agree.

Nominate Officers

Week 4

👫👫 whole class   🕐 30–60 minutes

Materials: none

According to the rules on which students have agreed, hold a nominating session for class officers. Because there are no officers yet, you or a volunteer may preside.

Hold an Election

Weeks 5 & 6

👫👫 whole class   🕐 30–40 minutes

Materials: chart paper or craft paper, marker

Hold an election by a show of hands or by secret ballot. Following the election, one of the officers should write down the agreed-upon procedures and rules in large letters on chart or craft paper. Then post them on a bulletin board under the heading, Our Class Constitution. For the next week, students should consider this constitution a guide for their actions in class. At the end of the week, discuss the constitution, allowing the students to keep or amend it.

Our Class Constitution

1. We will not interrrupt each other.

2. We will be polite to each other.

3. We will not take things without asking.

Winter Wonderland

It's hard to believe that the Northeast is the same place in the winter as it is in the summer, spring, or fall—especially if a snowstorm comes along!

The Parts: (4–5 players) • Five Students *(leaving school on a winter afternoon)*

Director's Notes: With your group, brainstorm what players might say about winter—how it looks and feels, what happens to animals and plants, and what you like and don't like about the coldest season of all.

(Players are wearing winter clothes. They look cold and walk as if moving through deep snow.)

Student 1: It's almost dark out, and it's not even four o'clock yet.

Student 2: Want to know why? *(**Improv Directions:** Explain why it gets dark earlier in the winter than in other seasons.)*

Student 3: I see a few birds twittering about. But do you know what animals do in the winter? *(**Improv Directions:** Tells a few things about animals that hibernate.)*

Student 4: Sounds like some animals have found a way to get through the winter. But how do you think plants cope with the cold? *(**Improv Directions:** Talks about plants in winter.)*

Student 5: Well I can see how plants and animals adapt to the winter. But how about us human beings? I can tell you how I like to stay warm on a cold day. *(**Improv Directions:** Talks about ways to stay warm.)*

Student 1: It's cold and dark, but it's also beautiful when everything is covered with snow. *(**Improv Directions:** Talks about the beauty of the snow.)*

Student 2: Well, it's not dark yet. Let's play. What should we do? *(**Improv Directions:** All students discuss what they could do on this snowy winter afternoon.)*

Student 3: I vote for sledding. That's the most fun of all.

Student 4: Sledding is fun. But I'll still be happy when spring comes. No more heavy coats and boots! No more cold fingers.

Student 5: Come on everybody! Let's get our sleds and meet on the hill!

(Students run out laughing.)

© Scott Foresman 4

Hello, Sweet Spring!

Winter was fun, but now it seems as if the whole world is coming alive again. No more boots ...no more hats ...no more mittens. Spring has sprung!

The Parts: (4–5 players) • Five Students *(working in a garden)*

Director's Notes: With your group, brainstorm what players might say about how it feels when spring comes after a long, cold winter.

Student 1: *(pointing to tree branches above)* Look! The birds are coming back.

Student 2: *(also looking up)* And the trees are starting to get green again.

Student 3: *(pointing to the ground.)* Look at this! The daffodil bulbs we planted last fall are starting to come up.

Student 4: Great. *(Improv Directions: Talks about how it feels when spring comes and the long, cold winter is over at last.)*

Student 5: Remember when we planted these bulbs? We said we'd plant a vegetable garden in the spring.

Student 1: Right. If we wait for summer, it'll be too late. We'd better plant our seeds soon. *(Improv Directions: All talk about which vegetables they would like to plant.)*

Student 2: Before we plant seeds, we have to get the ground ready. We have to dig it up so it will be nice and soft.

Student 3: We could do that right now. *(Improv Directions: All students pick up real or imaginary shovels and start digging up the garden.)*

Student 4: Be careful not to dig up our daffodils!

Student 5: Can you believe it's five o'clock, and the sun hasn't set yet? We still have plenty of time to work.

Student 1: Soon it will be summer. Then we can go swimming and play outside until seven or eight. *(Improv Directions: All improvise about looking forward to summer.)*

Summer and Fall

Summer means fun. School is out, and there's plenty of time to play. Then comes fall, and the Northeast is ablaze with color.

The Parts: (4–5 players) • Five Students

 Director's Notes: With your group, brainstorm what players might say about how they feel and what they like to do in summer and fall.

Student 1: *(to the audience)* School's out! It's summer! *(Joins other students sitting under a shade tree.)*

Student 2: I don't know about you, but I'm too hot to do anything.

Student 3: *(Improv Directions: Talks about feeling hot on summer days.)*

Student 4: I don't care if it's hot. I wish it could be summer all the time. It's my favorite season. *(Improv Directions: Talks about loving summer.)*

Student 5: You'd have to live near the equator to have warm weather all the time.

Student 1: I like living in the Northeast, because every season is different.

Student 2: Right. Before you know it, the leaves will start to turn color and it will be fall. And we'll be back in school.

Student 3: Well, it's summer now, so let's get our bathing suits. *(Student 1 stays while the other players walk stage right.)*

Student 1: *(to the audience)* Well, it was a great summer. Now fall is here. *(Looks up and around at the trees.)* This is a great day for a hike. Look at the colors of those leaves!

Student 2: Fall is beautiful, but I hate when summer ends. No more swimming, no more long days.

Student 3: I love the fall, but it always makes me feel a little sad. Soon there won't be any leaves left on the trees.

Student 4: When fall begins, you know that winter's coming soon.

Student 5: That's true. But then what happens? Spring comes again.

© Scott Foresman 4

Explore the Northeast

Explore the places of the varied Northeast and explore
the philosophy of one of its native writers when you
stage these scenarios.

Roger Williams Visits the Grand Sachem

Stage the scene when Roger Williams first visited the Grand
Sachem of the Narragansett people, Canonicus. How does he
try to establish friendly relations with the Native Americans?
What does he want from them? How do they react? Have they
ever seen a European before?

The British Surrender!

General George Washington has
defeated the British general, Lord
Cornwallis at Yorktown. The British
have surrendered! The war is over! The
colonies have really won their
independence! Stage the scene as the
news spreads through the Northeast that
the war is over and the colonies have won!
What are people's reactions? Is everyone
happy? Who is and who is not? What are
some of the concerns people have about how
things will work now that Britain is no longer
the ruler? What are the hopes of different
people for a land where people can be truly free
and equal?

The Abolitionists

Choose one of the following well-known figures in the 19th
century fight against slavery and do some research on the
person's life: Frederick Douglass, Sojourner Truth, Harriet
Tubman. Stage a scene from the life of the person, or you
might want to give a dramatic reading from one of their
speeches.

Explore the Northeast _continued_

Women Speak Out

Before the 1900s, women in the United States did not have the right to vote. They also did not have many other rights that men had. In the 1800s, reformers began to fight for women's rights. Research the lives of one of the following reformers and look for an important moment in their life that you could stage: Elizabeth Cady Stanton, Lucretia Mott, Susan B. Anthony. You might want to stage the first women's rights convention that took place in Seneca Falls, New York. Write your own version of the women's declaration of rights that was read at that convention. What did these women want? What arguments did they give in favor of equal rights for women and men?

Walden Pond

Henry David Thoreau, a native son of Massachusetts, was a writer who decided to try to live a simple life on the land. In 1845, he built himself a cabin in the woods near Walden Pond and went to live there alone. His book _Walden_ is a record of his thoughts as he watched the seasons change.

Stage the scene where Thoreau explains to his friends why he is going off to live alone in nature. Why does he want to do this? Why does he feel the pace of modern life is becoming too fast? How does he feel about inventions such as the railroad and the telegraph? What kind of life is he seeking?

Social Studies Plus!

A Land of Promise

From its very beginning, the United States has been a land of immigrants. Suppose that you and your family are immigrants, either today, or in some time from the past. Decide what time you want to be from, where you are coming from, and why you have decided to leave your native land and come to the U.S. Suppose that you arrive in one of the cities of the Northeast. What are your first impressions? How will you deal with this new land?

All Aboard!

A group of tourists from different countries has signed up for a bus tour of the Northeast. Work together in a group to decide the itinerary for your tour. Decide which students will play the tour guides. You might want to have a separate tour guide for each city you visit. Each of the other students should decide which country he or she comes from. Then stage the tour.

What questions would each tourist ask at each stop? What would be of most interest to different tourists? What can the tour guides tell about the history and natural resources of each place? Use these questions as a guide for brainstorming and improvising your scene.

Short-Term Projects

The Northeast is a veritable feast of plenty of things to see and do. Here are some things your students can do to deepen their appreciation of this fascinating region.

Make a Model
partners — **40 minutes**

Materials: cardboard or oaktag, clay or homemade play dough, paints, paintbrushes

1. Start out by encouraging your students to talk about the different land forms and water forms they have read about in the chapter—glacier, gorge, peninsula, bay, and inlet.

2. Assign one of the forms to each pair so that they may begin making models.

3. Give students time to plan how they will make their models and gather their materials.

4. Give students time to mold and paint their models. Display the finished models in the classroom.

Power Flow
individual — **20 minutes**

Materials: large sheets of paper, crayons or markers

Direct students' attention to the cross-section diagram and explanation of a hydropower plant on pages 110–111 of their textbooks. Explain that a cross-section diagram is one way of showing how something works. Another way is a flow chart. Have students make flow charts that show how a hydropower plant produces electricity. Guide students to recognize the sequence of events described in their textbooks and to use arrows to connect each step in their flow charts.

Calling All Leaf Peepers!
individual — **20 minutes**

Materials: large sheets of paper or oaktag, crayons, markers, paints, paintbrushes

Autumn draws a flood of tourists to the Northeast, because no other part of the United States puts on such a dramatic show of colors at this time of year. The many tourists who visit the Northeast to see the autumn foliage have a name—"leaf peepers." Invite your students to create travel posters that invite people to come to the Northeast to see and share autumn in all its glory.

© Scott Foresman 4

What Will You Have?

👫 group   **🕐 20 minutes**

Materials: paper; pencils, crayons or markers

Students have learned that the Chesapeake Bay is known for the three kinds of shellfish harvested there—oysters, clams, and crabs. Let them know that the Chesapeake Bay area is also known for its many restaurants that specialize in serving these types of shellfish and other seafood. Invite groups to create their own menus for a seafood restaurant in the Chesapeake Bay area. Students may wish to write their menus with their restaurant's name on folded paper and illustrate the menus to make them look more authentic.

Give Me Your Tired

👨‍👩 group   **🕐 45 minutes**

Materials: copies of "The New Colossus," by Emma Lazarus

On the base of the Statue of Liberty is the famous poem "The New Colossus" by Emma Lazarus. The sight of the Statue of Liberty has welcomed many immigrants to the United States, and the poem speaks of the opportunities for a better life these people hoped to find here.

Have a group of students present the poem to the class in choral readings. Each student in the group can read a small section of the poem, or the whole group can read it together.

Remember! Keep working on that Long-Term Project.

Bay Watchers

👫 partners   **🕐 15 minutes**

Materials: none

Students have learned that overfishing has caused the Chesapeake Bay Foundation to try to stop it. Ask students to imagine that environmentalists are trying to get laws passed that limit the number of fish that may be taken from the bay. Why might fishermen oppose such laws? How would environmentalists argue? Invite partners to debate each side of the issue. Encourage partners to share any conclusions they draw with the class.

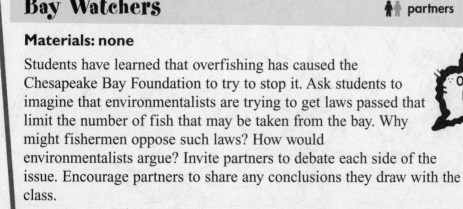

OVERFISHING IS BAD FOR THE BAY!

WE NEED TO MAKE A LIVING!

Writing Projects

The Northeast—what a great place to live! Encourage students to use written expression to broaden their view of what makes the Northeast great.

Appalachian Poem

Students have read about the Appalachian Trail, which reaches from Maine all the way to Georgia. Let them know that many people hike sections of the trail and that some people have actually hiked the entire length of the Appalachian Trail. Invite students to suppose that they are hikers on the trail and write short poems about their experiences—what they see and hear and how they feel.

Pen Pal Letter

In climates nearer the equator—the Southeast or Southwest, for example—people do not experience the weather and sights of autumn and winter. Some people have lived all their lives in southern climates and have never experienced a Northeast winter or autumn. Have students make up letters as if they were sending them to pen pals who have never experienced a real autumn or winter. In their letters, students should describe autumn or winter in the Northeast. Remind students to use vivid adjectives to make their descriptions come alive.

Is It a Berry?

Remind students that grapes and cranberries are two types of berries grown in the Northeast. Explain to students that a berry is any fruit in which the seeds are distributed throughout the fruit (for example, an orange) rather than contained in a core or pit (for example, a pear). List the following fruits on the chalkboard: raspberry, apple, peach, tomato, plum, banana, lemon, and cherry.

Have students write their own definitions of a berry and classify the fruits on the list as berries or nonberries. They should also write a sentence that indicates which of these fruits grow in the Northeast.

Then have students edit and revise their work after checking it against your answers. (Berries: raspberry, tomato, banana, lemon. Nonberries: apple, peach, plum, cherry. Northeast fruits: raspberry, apple, peach, tomato, plum, cherry.)

A Weekend Trip

There are so many vacation spots in the Northeast. People visit the White Mountains, Green Mountains, and Catskills to ski and hike; they relax and swim at beaches on Cape Cod and on the New Jersey shore; they visit cities such as Boston, Philadelphia, and New York for entertainment and sightseeing. Invite students to research a vacation spot they would like to visit in the Northeast and write schedules for a two-day weekend trip. Students' schedules should show what they plan to do at different times during each day of the trip.

Chapter 4 Citizenship

Caring

We all care about things that are important to us. But students need to learn that *doing* is part of caring.

On the chalkboard, write "I care about . . ." Ask students to think of different ways to complete the sentence by brainstorming things that are important to them. Write their suggestions on the chalkboard. Then lead students to develop a definition of the word *caring*. Help students to understand that caring is more than just worrying about something or feeling that something is important. Real caring involves a willingness to act.

Go back to the list that students created. Ask them to think of things that they could do to show that they care about the things on the list. Remind them that even small things are important.

Encourage students to work individually or in a group to plan projects that show caring through action. The projects can be as simple as students helping at home to show they care about families or spending time helping a younger child with homework to show they care about education. After students have made their plans, they should put them into action for a week and then write about their experiences. They can use blackline master on page 45 to plan their projects and write about them.

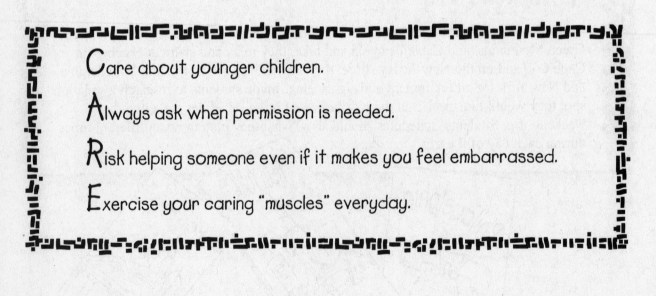

Care about younger children.

Always ask when permission is needed.

Risk helping someone even if it makes you feel embarrassed.

Exercise your caring "muscles" everyday.

Social Studies Plus!

Caring in Action

Write down three things you care about and the ways you can show that you care. Then choose one of the things you wrote about. Spend the next week doing things that show that you care.

1. I care about _____

I can show I care by _____

_____

2. I care about _____

I can show I care by _____

_____

3. I care about _____

I can show I care by _____

_____

Write about your experiences after the week is over.

_____

_____

_____

_____

_____

_____

_____

_____

_____

Great, towering cities, diverse populations, historic places in the birth of our nation—these also are the riches of the Northeast. Hands-on projects help students to further explore this rich region.

The Narragansett Way

👥 group   🕐 20 minutes

Materials: paper, pencils

The society of the Narragansett people was based on cooperation and sharing rather than on competition. Neighbors helped each other whenever there was a need. Discuss with students how the classroom can better reflect the community spirit of the Narragansett. Invite students to make a list of the ways in which they can cooperate with each other. Ideas might include sharing supplies or helping tutor younger students with homework assignments.

> Remember!
> Keep working
> on that
> Long-Term Project.

Wigwam Models

👤 partners   🕐 20 minutes

Materials: pipe cleaners, tape, fabric or tissue paper, scissors

The Narragansett people lived in wigwams—a dome-shaped structure made from layers of bark draped over a frame of poles. Find a picture to show students and suggest they build their own model wigwams based on the illustration.

1. Use pipe cleaners as poles and tape them together at the top.

2. Cover the poles with fabric or tissue paper.

3. Cut an opening in the fabric or paper to make a doorway.

Display the finished models in the classroom.

© Scott Foresman 4

History Trail

👥 partners   🕐 20 minutes

Materials: copies of road maps of the Northeast, markers, pencils, paper

There are so many historical places to see in the Northeast. Have students suppose they are going to take a trip to visit three sites of important historical events that took place in the Northeast. On a map of the region, have them draw a route they could follow, circling each place they would visit. On a sheet of paper students should list each site and the events that happened there. They might start at Lexington, Massachusetts (first battle of the American Revolution), proceed to New York City (the first capital of the United States), and end up in Philadelphia (where of the Declaration of Independence was signed).

"Concord Hymn"

👥👥 whole class/individual 👤   🕐 20 minutes

Materials: chalkboard, paper, pencils, crayons

The poem "Concord Hymn," by Ralph Waldo Emerson, describes the first battle of the American Revolution. Invite students to read the first stanza of the poem after you write it on the chalkboard and suggest illustrating it later on paper.

> By the rude bridge that arched the flood,   Here once the embattled farmers stood
> Their flag to April's breeze unfurled,   And fired the shot heard round the world.

Discuss with students the phrase "the shot heard round the world," leading them to understand that the American Revolution had important influence on world history.

Help Wanted

👥 partners   🕐 20 minutes

Materials: "Help Wanted" section of a local newspaper, scissors, construction paper, glue or paste

The availability of jobs is one of the factors that makes people want to live in a certain area. It is certainly one of the factors that brought so many people to the Northeast. Invite partners to look over the "Help Wanted" section of a local newspaper and discuss jobs that interest them. Then have students cut out the ads, paste them onto construction paper, and display them under the heading, Great Jobs in Our Own Backyard.

HELP WANTED

Writing Projects

Sharpen those pencils! It's time for students to hone their writing skills by further exploring the people and history of the Northeast.

Immigrant's Journal

Ask students to suppose that they are immigrants from another country during one of the three major waves of immigration to the United States. They have left their homes, friends, and families. They do not speak English, they have never been to the United States before, and they do not know what they will find here. But they hope for better lives than the ones they left behind. Have students write journal entries telling how they feel as they sail into New York Harbor and see the Statue of Liberty for the first time.

Native American Place Names

Many places in the Northeast have names that come from Native American languages. Most of these names describe the places, or tell what they are like. Massachusetts, for example, means "the place of the great hill"; Chesapeake Bay means "great shellfish bay"; and Connecticut means "long river." Have students make up new names in English for places with which they are familiar. Their names should tell what the places look like. For example, they might name a large city Place of Tall Buildings or a town near a lake Village on the Water. Students can share their place names and challenge classmates to guess the real names of the places they describe.

CHESAPEAKE BAY

© Scott Foresman 4

Lecture Summary: The Iroquois Constitution

Tell students that more than two hundred years before the United States became a nation, the Five Nations of the Iroquois Confederacy (the Cayuga, Mohawk, Oneida, Onondaga, and Seneca tribes) joined together to gain strength and agree upon a constitution. Tell the students you are going to give a short lecture on the Iroquois government, and invite them to take notes. Afterward, they will use their notes to write summaries of the lecture.

In your lecture, explain that each of the five Iroquois nations sent representatives to a great federation council to make laws for the confederacy and settle arguments. Each nation included several groups, or clans, and each clan had a chief. Because every chief attended meetings of the Confederacy, the nations with more clans were represented by more chiefs than were the smaller nations. The Iroquois constitution ensured equality among smaller and larger nations of the confederacy by giving each nation only one vote on confederacy issues. Clan chiefs, therefore, had to agree before casting a vote for their nation. Invite volunteers to read their summaries aloud to the class.

Tale of Two Cities

Encourage students to compare and contrast the Northeast's three biggest cities: New York, Boston, and Philadelphia with their own town or city. Suggest a graphic organizer for student partners to compare and contrast population, area, and main businesses. Students may need to do some additional research to complete this project.

Citizenship

Respect

Students often hear that they should have respect—for older people, for teachers, for parents. This activity helps students see that *everyone* deserves respect, no matter his or her age or position.

Begin a discussion of respect with your class by asking students to consider what it means to disrespect someone. Students may say that when you disrespect others, you insult them, criticize them harshly, make fun of them, speak rudely to them, or simply ignore them. Move on by asking students to focus on how they feel when they are disrespected. You can then lead students to conclude that since they don't like to be disrespected, they should not treat others that way.

Students may now go on to consider the opposite question: How do we show respect for others? Invite students to list ways of showing respect for others in a variety of situations: in class, in sports, at home, and in public places such as stores, buses, and movie theaters. Invite groups of students to role-play situations such as the following to show examples of both disrespectful and respectful behavior. Then have them fill in the speech balloons on the blackline master on page 51.

1. A student acting in a school play forgets his or her lines in the middle of a performance.

2. Your soccer team wins a game against another team.

3. A student in your class gives the wrong answer to a question your teacher has asked.

© Scott Foresman 4

Name _____ Date _____

Words of Respect

In each cartoon, fill in the empty speech balloon with one or more words that show respectful behavior.

Teacher Planner

Long-Term Project pages 54–55	Materials	🕐	Lesson Link
Come on Down! Students create travel brochures about the great Southeast.			Lessons 1–3
Week 1 👤👤👤 whole class Students brainstorm places they would like to visit in the Southeast.	none	1 session 20 min.	
Week 2 👤👤👤 group Students collect images of the Southeast from newspapers, magazines, or the Internet.	pencils, note cards	1 session 30–40 min	
Weeks 3 & 4 👤👤👤 group Students arrange their pictures on their brochures.	pictures of places in the Southeast, art supplies	1 session 30–40 min.	
Week 5 👤👤👤 whole class Students create covers for their brochures.	brochure pages from Weeks 3 and 4	1 session 45 min.	

Unit Drama pages 56–61			
Scenarios: Successes and Defeats 👤👤👤 group Students role-play skits about the hardships and triumphs of settlers and presidents.	props (optional)	3 sessions 30 min. each	Lessons 1–3
Play: Two Sides of a Story: Acts 1 and 2 👤👤👤 group Students perform a play about the South during the Civil War.	props, costumes (optional)	1 session 1 hr.	Lessons 1–3
Play: Two Sides of a Story: Acts 3 and 4 👤👤👤 group Students perform a play about slavery during the Civil War.	props , costumes (optional)	1 session 1 hr.	Lessons 1–3

Chapter 6 Short-Term Projects pages 62–63			
Make a Relief Map 👤👤 partners Students create relief maps of the Southeast.	cardboard or oaktag, clay, paints and brushes	1 session 30 min.	Lessons 1–3
Label It! 👤👤👤 group Students make up brand names and labels for Southeast products.	paper, crayons, markers, scissors	1 session 20 min.	Lessons 1–3
It Comes from Trees 👤 individual Students create a web-type graphic organizer to represent things that are made from trees.	construction paper, crayons, markers	1 session 20 min.	Lesson 3
Southeast Jam Session 👤 individual Students find and listen to examples of different types of music that originated in the American Southeast.	cassette or CD player, music recordings	1 session 30–45 min.	Lesson 3
Alligators and Company 👤 individual Students find names of pictures of animals in the Everglades.	paper, markers, crayons	1 session 20 min.	Lesson 3

© Scott Foresman 4

Chapter 6 Writing Projects pages 64–65	Materials	🕐	Lesson Link
Describe a Beautiful Place 👤 individual Students write descriptions of what they see in photographs of different environments of the Southeast.	paper, pencils	1 session 20 min.	Lessons 1–3
Persuasive Paragraph 👤 individual Students write letters to persuade their friends to visit them in the Southeast during the winter.	paper, pencils	1 session 30 min.	Lessons 1–3
Hurricane Warning! 👤 individual Students write instructions informing people living in the Southeast what safety measures to take when a hurricane strikes.	paper, pencils	1 session 25 min.	Lesson 2
The Useful Peanut 👤 individual Students write paragraphs about the many uses of peanuts.	paper, pencils	1 session 20 min.	Lesson 3
Chapter 6 Citizenship Project page 66			
Caring 👤👤👤 whole class Students are challenged to care about the earth and our environment.	BLM p. 67, paper, pencils	1 session 40 min.	Lessons 1–3
Chapter 7 Short-Term Projects pages 68–69			
Creating an Alphabet 👤👤 partners Students make up symbols to stand for syllables in several common words in English.	paper, pencils	1 session 20 min.	Lesson 1
Cherokee House Models 👤👤 partners Students make models of the rectangular houses the Cherokee used in warm weather.	oaktag, construction paper, craft sticks, scissors, tape	1 session 30 min.	Lesson 1
Everyone Agrees! 👤👤👤 whole class/partners 👤👤 Students debate issues in order to reach a consensus.	note cards, pencils	1 session 20 min.	Lesson 1
Explorer Chart 👤 individual Students make a chart comparing the explorers' countries of origin.	paper, pencils	1 session 20 min.	Lesson 2
Build a Spanish Fort 👤👤 partners Students make their own fort modeled on Castillo de San Marcos.	clay, craft sticks, picture of Castillo de San Marcos	1 session 30 min.	Lesson 2
What's the Weather? 👤 individual Students find the temperature for the day in several Southeast cities.	major newspaper with national forecast, paper, pencils	1 session 20 min.	Lessons 3–4
Chapter 7 Writing Projects pages 70–71			
Original Legends 👤 individual Students create their own legends of wonderful places that people might want to search for.	paper, pencils	1 session 25 min.	Lesson 2

Chapter 7 Writing Projects *continued*	Materials	🕐	Lesson Link
The Lost Colony 🧍 individual Students suggest why the colony of Roanoke Island disappeared.	paper, pencils	1 session 20 min.	Lesson 2
Southeastern Architecture 🧍 individual Students write imaginary accounts of a visit to Monticello in 1810.	paper, pencils	1 session 20 min.	Lesson 2
King of the Wild Frontier 🧍 individual Students write their own legend about a person they have learned about in the chapter.	paper, pencils	1 session 25 min.	Lesson 2
Southeastern Presidents 🧍 individual Students write biographical sentences about a president born in the Southeast.	paper, pencils	1 session 20 min.	Lesson 2–3 Lesson 3
The Words of Dr. Martin Luther King, Jr. 🧍 individual Students write their own "I have a dream" speeches.	paper, pencils	1 session 30 min.	

Chapter 7 Citizenship Project page 72			
Courage 🧍🧍🧍 whole class Students share stories about courageous people they have known.	BLM p. 73, paper, pencils	1 session 40 min.	Lessons 1–4

NOTES

_____

_____

_____

_____

_____

_____

_____

_____

_____

_____

_____

_____

_____

_____

_____

_____

_____

_____

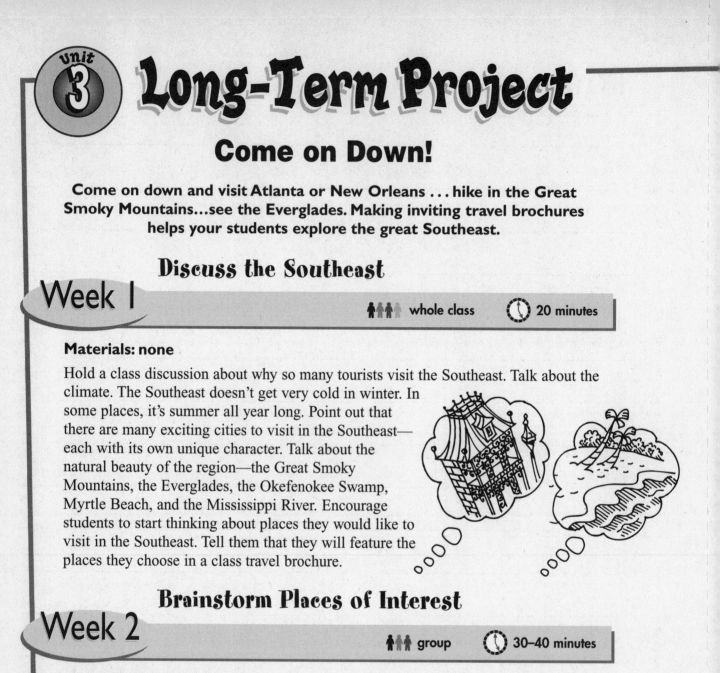

Unit 3 Long-Term Project

Come on Down!

Come on down and visit Atlanta or New Orleans . . . hike in the Great Smoky Mountains...see the Everglades. Making inviting travel brochures helps your students explore the great Southeast.

Discuss the Southeast

Week 1

👫👫 whole class   🕐 20 minutes

Materials: none

Hold a class discussion about why so many tourists visit the Southeast. Talk about the climate. The Southeast doesn't get very cold in winter. In some places, it's summer all year long. Point out that there are many exciting cities to visit in the Southeast—each with its own unique character. Talk about the natural beauty of the region—the Great Smoky Mountains, the Everglades, the Okefenokee Swamp, Myrtle Beach, and the Mississippi River. Encourage students to start thinking about places they would like to visit in the Southeast. Tell them that they will feature the places they choose in a class travel brochure.

Brainstorm Places of Interest

Week 2

👫👫 group   🕐 30–40 minutes

Materials: pencils, note cards

Divide the class into groups. Set aside time for groups to hold brainstorming sessions in which they list places of interest in the Southeast that they know or have heard about.

Allow them to do some preliminary research. Students should write the name of each place they come up with on a note card, with a few words to describe or identify it. Collect the cards, discard duplicates, and divide the remaining cards among the groups. The places on the cards each group receives will be the ones the members will write about for the class brochure.

Suggest that students collect from home images of the Southeast from newspapers or magazines or ask an adult to help them download images from the Internet. They should bring these images to class to use during Weeks 3 and 4.

© Scott Foresman 4

Create the Brochure

Weeks 3 & 4

👤👤👤 group   🕐 30–40 minutes

Materials: pictures of places in the Southeast, magazines, travel brochures, pencils, crayons, markers, white or colored paper, scissors, paste or glue

Working together in their groups, students can now create their portions of the class brochure by writing about and providing images of the places assigned to them. Students can draw pictures, use images they have collected from home, download images (with your help) from the Internet, or cut pictures out of magazines or travel brochures. Direct students to paste their pictures on paper, leaving room for captions. The captions should be brief and should tell why each place would be interesting or fun to visit. All students should use the same size paper so that the pages can be assembled into a travel brochure when the project is completed.

Visit Miami
Beach.
You can swim
in the ocean
all year round

Presentation Day

Week 5

👤👤👤 whole class   🕐 45 minutes

Materials: brochure pages from Weeks 3 and 4

Allow time for each group to present its work to the class. After the presentations, choose two or three volunteers to put all the pages of the brochure together and organize them by categories such as cities, vacation spots, and natural sights. Choose another volunteer or pair of students to create a cover for the brochure. Staple the pages together and display the completed brochure in the classroom where students can browse through it.

Successes and Defeats

Students use improvisation to bring alive the hardships and
triumphs of settlers and presidents! They improvise to prepare for
a play about the Civil War.

The Lost Colony

Suppose that you are part of the group
of 100 settlers who sailed from
England to establish a colony on
Roanoke Island in what is now
North Carolina. Improvise getting
off the ship after the long voyage.
What are your reactions to the land
you find? How do you think you will
survive? When your leader John
White leaves to get more supplies in
England, the colony has little food left.
What do you do? What happens? What
is the meaning of the word
"CROATOAN" that White finds
carved into a tree trunk when he
returns in 1590?

Four Early Presidents

Research and stage some scenes in the life of one of these
presidents: George Washington, Thomas Jefferson, James
Madison, or Andrew Jackson. What was one of the biggest
problems he faced? What was one of his greatest
achievements? Invent characters who might have known him,
or worked for him, or against him, to tell his story from their
own point of view.

© Scott Foresman 4

Acting Class

Tell students that they are about to fight a battle—a battle of words, that is. They will perform a play called Both Sides of a Story, in which characters from the North and the South express their different views on the Civil War and the issues that surrounded it. Remind students that some of them will play characters that express views that are different from students' own views. Doing this may seem hard at first, but playing the part of someone who is different from oneself is an important part of acting.

Inform students that as a warm-up to the play, they will improvise discussions in which they express views on current issues. The exercises will give them practice in defending opinions—even if those opinions are not ones that they agree with.

Form groups. Give the groups a little time to brainstorm issues on which people have different views. Such as the following:

• Should students be allowed to wear anything they want to school, or should there be a dress code or school uniforms?

• Should people younger than eighteen be allowed to vote?

• Should school be required by law, or should parents decide whether their child should attend school?

Have group members write the issues they come up with on note cards—one issue per card. Collect the cards, mix them together, and have a member of each group pick one card.

Give each group a few moments to decide which members will take which side of the group's issue. Remind students that, whether improvising or reading from a script, a person in a drama is playing the part of a character—not himself or herself. Then have groups improvise a discussion about its issue in front of the rest of the class. As they improvise, students should try to give the strongest arguments possible for the opinions they have been called upon to defend.

After each group's improvisation, allow time for some feedback or constructive criticism from the rest of the class.

Two Sides of a Story

How much power should the federal government have over the states? And if slavery is outlawed, how will people in the South make a living?

Act 1–The Seeds of War

The Parts:

(4 players)
- Narrator 1
- Narrator 3
- Narrator 2
- Narrator 4

Director's Notes: The play begins with four narrators telling how the Civil War began. Narrators may memorize or read their parts or use the script to improvise, or make up, what they will say. With your group, decide whether each narrator will memorize, read, or improvise.

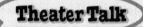

Theater Talk

act: one of the main divisions of a play

narrator: player who speaks directly to the audience about what is going on in the drama

Narrator 1: Let us take you back to the year 1860. The Civil War is about to begin. Some people call it the War between the States. In this war, citizens of the United States will fight against their fellow citizens. Some soldiers will even fight members of their own families. This war will be between the Northern states and the Southern states.

Narrator 2: In the South, people have slaves. But people in the North think that slavery is wrong. They think that the federal government should make a law against slavery. And they think that all states must follow the laws of the federal government.

© Scott Foresman 4

Narrator 3: People in the South say that they need slaves. They think that the federal government should not be able to tell the Southern states what to do. Each state should make its own decision.

Narrator 4: Abraham Lincoln has been elected President of the United States. He thinks that the federal government should have more power. The Southern states decide to secede, or separate, from the United States. Lincoln says they can't do that. The war is about to begin.

Act 2–View from the South

The Parts: (5 players, group of Southern citizens)
- Citizen 1
- Citizen 2
- Citizen 3
- Citizen 4
- Citizen 5

Director's Notes: Some players will memorize their parts. Other players will improvise, or make up, their lines. In a group of three, brainstorm what players might say about slavery, Abraham Lincoln, the North, and seceding from the United States of America. Read your textbook to get ideas.

Tell your players to watch for stage directions in the play. They are shown in parentheses.

(*Citizens are standing on a street corner in a small town in the South.*)

Citizen 1: What will happen now that Lincoln is President?

Citizen 2: (*Improv Directions: Give opinion on what Lincoln will do about slavery.*)

Citizen 3: Lincoln has no right to outlaw slavery! (*Improv Directions: Give opinion against the federal government's power over the states.*)

Citizen 4: I say if slavery is abolished, we should start our own country and make our own laws.

Citizen 5: And what would we do about slavery? I can't really say that I like it.

All: (*Improv Directions: Give thoughts about slavery, agreeing or disagreeing.*)

Citizen 1: Well, do we secede or don't we?

Citizen 2: I'm afraid that we must. And we'll have to fight to do it!

Two Sides of a Story

If slavery is wrong, how can the federal government let it exist? Can the United States survive if states can just drop out of the union whenever they want?

Act 3—The View from the North

The Parts:

(5 players)
- Citizen 1
- Citizen 2
- Citizen 3
- Citizen 4
- Citizen 5

Director's Notes: Some players will memorize their parts. Other players will improvise, or make up, their lines. In a group of three, brainstorm what players might say about slavery, Abraham Lincoln, and what will happen if the South secedes. Read your textbook to get ideas.

Tell your players to watch for stage directions in the play. They are shown in parentheses.

(Citizens are sitting in the living room of someone's home.)

Citizen 1: What will happen now that Lincoln's been elected? What do you think the South will do?

Citizen 2: The South might secede from the Union.

Citizen 3: Lincoln will never stand for that. It'll mean war! *(Improv Directions: Give thoughts about why the federal government can't allow the South to secede.)*

Citizen 4: And what about slavery? It's just wrong! It goes against everything our country stands for!

All: *(Improv Directions: Add thoughts on why slavery is wrong.)*

Citizen 5: The Southerners say they can't make a living without slaves.

Citizen 1: The point isn't how the South will survive. The point is that we can't allow slavery to exist and we can't allow the South to secede!

PLAYBILL

CIVIL WAR

A Two-Sided STORY

© Scott Foresman 4

Act 4—What Happens Next?

The Parts: (5 players)
- Narrator 1
- Narrator 3
- Narrator 5
- Narrator 2
- Narrator 4

Director's Notes: In this part of the play, there is audience participation, that is, the audience will interact with the players. Members of the audience will be asked to explain what happened next. In a group of three, decide whether each narrator will memorize, read, or improvise. Suggest that narrators read about the Civil War in their textbooks to prepare to lead the discussion and answer questions from the audience.

Narrator 1: As we all know, the Civil War began in 1861 and lasted for four terrible years. Can someone in the audience tell us about the beginning of the war? *(Eleven Southern states seceded. They formed the Confederate States of America. President Lincoln declared war on the Confederacy.*

Narrator 2: During the Civil War, many people suffered. In the South, many farms and even whole cities were destroyed. What finally happened after four years of fighting? *(The South surrendered.)*

Narrator 3: After the war, life changed in the South. What was the biggest change? *(Slavery was no longer allowed.)*

Narrator 4: People who had been enslaved were now free American citizens. But most African Americans were poor. The Southern states passed segregation laws. What does segregation mean? *(African Americans were separated from white people and not treated equally.)*

Narrator 5: It took almost a hundred years after the Civil War for Congress to make a law against segregation—the Civil Rights Act of 1964. What led up to this law? *(In the 1950s, the civil rights movement began.)*

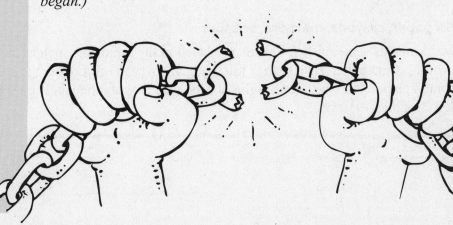

Short-Term Projects

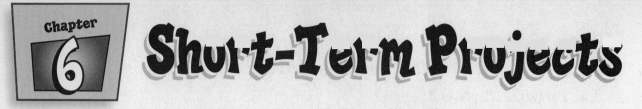

The Southeast is a region rich in natural resources and natural beauty. The following hands-on projects invite your students to further explore this warm and welcoming region.

Make a Relief Map

👫 partners   🕐 30 minutes

Materials: cardboard or oaktag, clay or homemade play dough (colorless), paints, paintbrushes

Direct partners' attention to the elevation map of the Southeast on page 170 of their student text. Explain that a *relief map* is a three-dimensional map that shows elevation. That is, it is built up to show what an area really looks like. Tell students that they can use the information on the elevation map to make their own relief maps of the Southeast out of clay.

Partners may use cardboard or oaktag as a base for their relief maps. The first layer of clay will represent the lowest elevations on the elevation map. Then they will build up additional layers to represent each higher elevation. When they are finished, their maps will show plains, hills, and mountains.

When the relief maps have dried, students may paint them in the manner of the color elevation map.

Label It!

👪 group   🕐 20 minutes

Materials: paper, crayons, markers, scissors

Review with students some of the products produced in the Southeast such as cotton clothing, corn, peanut butter, rice, orange juice, sugar, soybean oil. Encourage students to make up brand names and labels for Southeast products. Display the labels on a bulletin board titled "Southeast Harvest."

© Scott Foresman 4

It Comes from Trees

👤 individual   🕐 20 minutes

Materials: construction paper, crayons, markers

Many products of the Southeast come from trees—furniture, paper, and lumber, for example. Trees also cool the earth, provide homes for animals, and give off oxygen. Have partners create a web-type graphic organizer with a picture of a tree in the center and arrows pointing outward to pictures or words that represent things that are made from trees or benefits that trees provide. Display students' work on a bulletin board titled "Thanks to the Trees."

Southeast Jam Session

👤 individual   🕐 30–45 minutes

Materials: audio tape player or CD player, music recordings

The Southeast was home to several types of American music—jazz, country, bluegrass, and blues. Invite students to find and listen to examples of one or more of these types of music. Check your public library. Here are some suggestions:

- jazz: Louis Armstrong, Jellyroll Morton, Sidney Bechet
- country: the Stanley Brothers, the Carter Family, Tammy Wynette
- bluegrass: Earl Scruggs, Roy Acuff
- blues: Robert Johnson, Muddy Waters

Remember!
Keep working
on that
Long-Term Project.

Alligators and Company

👤 individual   🕐 20 minutes

The alligator is only one of many kinds of animals living in the Everglades— the vast area of wetlands in Florida. Others include crocodiles, manatees, huge turtles, and many species of birds. Have students do research to find names and pictures of animals of the Everglades and show several of them in labeled drawings. Exhibit their drawings on a bulletin board titled "The Everglades: Where the Wild Things Are."

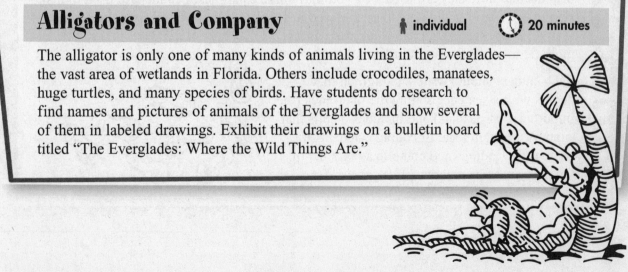

Writing Projects

Students are finding out about the Southeast's importance to the country as a whole. Here are some opportunities for them to share their discoveries through written expression.

Describe a Beautiful Place

Invite students to view photographs of different environments of the Southeast from your classroom library. Ask them to choose the photographs that they find most appealing.

Then have each student choose one photograph and write a description of what he or she sees in the photograph. Encourage students to use their imaginations to add details about how the place might smell, sound, and feel. Remind students that descriptive writing should use vivid language—especially vivid adjectives—to make a place seem real to the reader.

The Useful Peanut

Students have learned that an important product of the Southeast is the peanut. Everyone knows we can eat peanuts out of their shells and that many people love peanut butter sandwiches. Invite students to do research to find out more about peanuts and how they are used. (Or you may share examples: peanuts are used to make peanut oil, soaps, and paints; they are used in feed for livestock and to make certain textile fibers; and peanut shells are used as an ingredient in plastics and fertilizers.)

Each student should write a paragraph that begins with a sentence stating the main idea (the importance of peanuts) and includes details that support the main idea. Encourage students to share their findings and compile a class list of the many uses of peanuts.

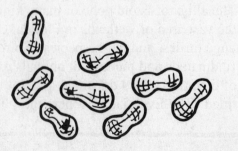

© Scott Foresman 4

Persuasive Paragraph

Have students suppose that they live in the Southeast and that they are writing letters to friends who live in climates that are cold in winter—the Northeast or the Midwest, for example. In their letters, students should try to persuade their friends to visit them in the Southeast during the winter. Writers can use warm climate, beautiful beaches, palm trees, colorful flowers, and other appealing features of the region as persuasive details. Remind students that persuasive writing should use language that convinces the reader to believe—and in this case, to act on—what the writer is saying.

Hurricane Warning!

With all of the Southeast's appealing qualities, there is one natural phenomenon common to this region that is destructive and dangerous—the hurricane. Guide students to research hurricanes to find out what causes them and what kind of damage they can do. Have students write, based on their research, sets of instructions informing people who live near the southeastern coast of the United States what safety measures to take when a hurricane strikes. Students may illustrate their lists with drawings and diagrams.

Citizenship

Caring

**How may we protect the beauty and wealth of the Southeast?
By caring, that's how. Bring apples to class to show students
why they should care about our fragile earth.**

Read students this quote from W. E. B. Du Bois: "Here is the magnificent climate, here is the fruitful earth under the beauty of the Southern sun..."

Challenge students to care about the earth and our environment as much as Du Bois cared about the South. Give an apple and a plastic knife to each student. Tell them that they will find out just how precious our natural resources are. Read the following dialogue to guide them through the activity.

"Let's imagine that your apple represents the earth.

"Cut the apple into quarters. Put aside three of the quarters. These represent the part of the earth that is water. The fraction that is left, one-quarter, represents the land.

"Slice the land quarter in half. Set aside one of the halves. The set aside part represents the land that people cannot live or work on, such as the North and South polar regions, deserts, swamps, and high mountains.

"What's left? One-eighth. This part represents where we humans live, but not exactly where we grow our food.

"Slice the one-eighth piece into four sections. Put aside three of them. What's left? One thirty-second. The three pieces you set aside represent the places where the soil is too poor to grow food—where it is too rocky, too wet, too cold, or too steep to farm. They also represent the cities, houses, highways, shopping malls, schools, parks, factories, parking lots, and swimming pools where people live, work, and play—but do not grow any food.

"Take the one thirty-second piece that is left. Carefully peel it. Set the flesh aside. Look at the scrap of apple peel. It represents the surface topsoil that may be farmed. The thin skin represents the earth's crust on which all living things depend. It is less than five feet deep. We cannot make more land. That is all there is.

"You may now eat and enjoy all of the apple pieces. Carefully save the tiny piece of apple skin. Treat the peel as if your life depends on it."

Before they eat their apples, you may want to invite students to complete the blackline master on page 67 to drive the lesson home.

© Scott Foresman 4

Eat Your Crust!

Did your apple help you to care more about the earth? Show what you learned.
Answer the following questions.

1. What fraction of the earth's surface is water?_____

2. What fraction of the earth's surface is land? _____

3. Name three places on the earth where people cannot live or work.

   a. _____

   b. _____

   c. _____

4. What are two places near where you live that are too rocky, too wet, too cold, or too steep to grow food?

   a. _____

   b. _____

5. Name two places, besides your home and school, where you have fun but cannot grow food.

   a. _____

   b. _____

6. Find a spot in your classroom that is five feet off the ground. This is how deep the topsoil is. How many people in your classroom are taller than this mark? _____

7. On the back of this paper, draw two pictures—one where you can grow food and one where you cannot grow food.

© Scott Foresman 4

Short-Term Projects

From the Cherokee to the European explorers, the early inhabitants of the Southeast present a rich tapestry. Tap that tapestry with these engaging activities.

Creating an Alphabet

👤👤 partners   🕐 20 minutes

Materials: paper, pencils

Explain to students that the Cherokee alphabet used symbols to stand for syllables of words. For example, whereas our letter *m* stands for the sound at the beginning of the word *missing*, the Cherokee alphabet would have a symbol that stood for the whole syllable *miss-* and another symbol that stood for the syllable *-ing*. These two symbols would spell the word *missing*. Invite partners to make up symbols to stand for syllables in several common words in English and to use their symbols to spell those words. They can trade alphabets with other pairs and see if they can "translate" each other's words.

Cherokee House Models

👤👤 partners   🕐 30 minutes

Materials: oaktag, construction paper, craft sticks, scissors, tape

Direct students to research and find pictures of Cherokee dwellings. Invite partners to make models of the rectangular houses the Cherokee used in warm weather. Students may put their models together to form a Cherokee village.

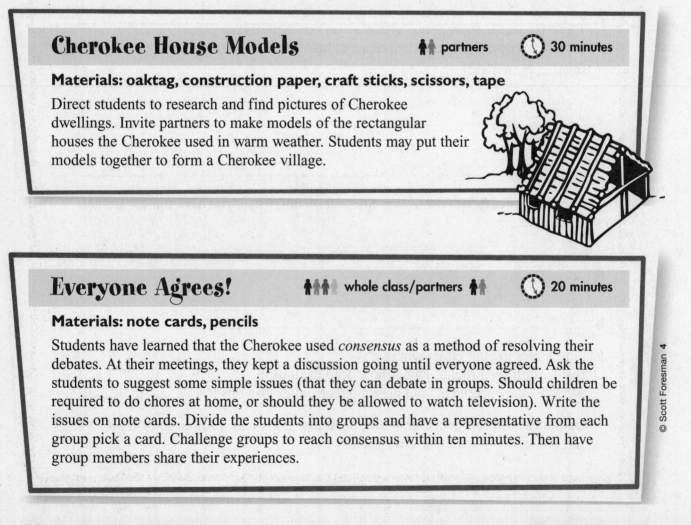

Everyone Agrees!

👤👤👤 whole class/partners 👤👤   🕐 20 minutes

Materials: note cards, pencils

Students have learned that the Cherokee used *consensus* as a method of resolving their debates. At their meetings, they kept a discussion going until everyone agreed. Ask the students to suggest some simple issues (that they can debate in groups. Should children be required to do chores at home, or should they be allowed to watch television). Write the issues on note cards. Divide the students into groups and have a representative from each group pick a card. Challenge groups to reach consensus within ten minutes. Then have group members share their experiences.

Explorer Chart

👤 individual   🕐 20 minutes

Materials: paper, pencils

Students have been reading about three explorers who came from Europe to the Southeast—Juan Ponce de León, Hernando de Soto, and Robert La Salle. Have students make a compare-and-contrast chart showing the explorers' countries of origin, the reasons for their expeditions, and what they accomplished.

Build a Spanish Fort

👥 partners   🕐 30 minutes

Materials: modeling clay, craft sticks, picture of Castillo de San Marcos

Castillo de San Marcos is the formidable stone fort built by the Spanish settlers in St. Augustine, Florida. Have students look at a picture of the fort. Point out the moat, the turret, and the huge blocks of stone. Invite partners to make their own fort modeled on Castillo de San Marcos. Students may use modeling clay to make their fort. They can use craft sticks to etch grids into the walls to represent the building stones.

> **Remember!
> Keep working
> on that
> Long-Term Project.**

What's the Weather?

👤 individual   🕐 20 minutes

Materials: major newspaper with national weather forecast, paper, pencils

Have students use the national weather forecast in a major newspaper to find the temperature for the day in several cities in the Southeast, such as Atlanta, Charleston, and Orlando. Invite them to compare the temperature in their own regions (or another region if they live in the Southeast). Have them show their findings in a bar graph.

Writing Projects

The people and history of the Southeast sometimes make the region seem larger than life. See if your students can distill the region's essence on paper.

Original Legends

Juan Ponce de León's search for the legendary Fountain of Youth led him to the land he named Florida. According to legend, those who drank from this fountain would live forever and be eternally young. Discuss with students why people would be willing to risk their lives to find such a place. Then invite students to create their own legends of wonderful places that people might want to search for. What are some things that are hard or impossible to get, but that most people would want?

The Lost Colony

Write about what happened to the "lost colony" of Roanoke Island. Ask students to suggest how the colony disappeared and why there was no trace of the settlers when John White returned from England. If students acted out the scenario of "The Lost Colony" from page 56, discuss being settlers on Roanoke Island and write diary entries explaining what happened to the colony. They might also offer their guesses as to the meaning of the word *CROATOAN,* which was found carved on a fence post.

Southeastern Presidents

Students have learned that the Presidents George Washington, Thomas Jefferson, James Madison, and Andrew Jackson were born in the Southeast. Tell the class that this region was also the birthplace of Presidents James K. Polk, Abraham Lincoln, Andrew Johnson, James Monroe, William Henry Harrison, John Tyler, Zachary Taylor, Woodrow Wilson, Jimmy Carter, and Bill Clinton. Have students choose a president born in the Southeast, do some research on him, and write a few biographical sentences about him. Students can contribute their sketches to a class book, "Presidents of the Southeast."

Southeastern Architecture

Invite students to research and find a photograph of Monticello, the home of Thomas Jefferson. Ask students to consider what it would be like to live in such a house. How many people would be required to manage the house? Who handled everyday chores such as planning the meals or dusting? What sorts of rooms besides the usual ones would be found in such a house? How was it heated? Invite students to write an imaginary account of a visit to Monticello in 1810.

King of the Wild Frontier

Many legends and tall tales grew up around the frontiersman Davy Crockett. Invite students to write their own legend about a real person they have learned about in this chapter, such as Daniel Boone, Sequoya, Ponce de León, or Sarah and Angelina Grimké. Remind students that legends combine truth with fiction.

The Words of Dr. Martin Luther King, Jr.

Dr. Martin Luther King, Jr., gave many speeches that are often quoted. The most famous of these is probably his "I have a dream…" speech. Distribute copies of the speech to students (available at http://douglass.speech.nwu.edu/ihaveadream.txt). Read the "I have a dream" section with students. Then ask students to think of something that would make the world a better place. Invite them to write their own "I have a dream" speech.

Citizenship

Courage

**What is courage? Is a courageous person someone who isn't afraid?
Or is it something else?**

Ask students to think of examples of courageous acts they have performed themselves, witnessed, heard about, or read about. List their examples on the chalkboard. Then invite students to use the examples they have contributed to write their own definition of courage. Ask them to include in their definition whether courage means never being afraid or whether it means being brave even when you're afraid.

Sarah and Angelina Grimké certainly showed courage in their opposition to slavery. Like the Grimké sisters, many people have had the courage to challenge prevailing ideas through word and deed. Ask students to think about people they have heard of or learned about who had the courage to stand up for what they believed in. You might cite people active in the American Revolution, the civil rights movement, the women's movement, and the labor movement as examples of individuals who stood up for their beliefs. Discuss with the class why these people needed courage. What did they have to fear? You may direct students to the biographical sketch of Rosa Parks on page 207 of Chapter 7 as an example.

Invite students to use the blackline master on page 73 to share stories about courageous people they have known, have read about in literature or history, or have encountered as characters in movies, on television, or even in songs. You may want to share their "Portraits in Courage" by posting them in a place that is accessible to the whole school.

© Scott Foresman 4

Portraits in Courage

Use the lines below to write about a person who showed true courage. The person can be someone that you know, someone you have read about in a book, or someone you have learned about in school. The person could even be a character in a movie, television show, or song.

What did the person do? Why do you think the person is courageous? Supply details.

_____

_____

_____

_____

_____

_____

_____

_____

_____

_____

_____

Teacher Planner

Long-Term Project pages 76–77	Materials	🕐	Lesson Link
Midwest Market Students make models of a supermarket stocked with Midwest goodies.			Lessons 1–3
Week 1 👥👥 whole class Students brainstorm a list of foods we get from the Midwest.	none	1 session 15 min.	
Week 2 👥👥 group Students plan how they will design containers, packages, and labels for their products.	index cards, paper, pencils	1 session 30–40 min.	
Week 3 & 4 👥👥 group Students create their packages for the supermarket.	cardboard, boxes, bags, empty cans, containers, art supplies	1 session 20–30 min.	
Week 5 👥👥 whole class Students present their products to the class.	students' containers and packages	1 session 20–30 min.	

Unit Drama pages 78–83			
Scenarios: Land Rush 👥👥 group Students role-play skits about moving into new homes .	props (optional)	2 sessions 40 min. each	Lessons 1–4
Play: Moving West 👥👥 group Students perform a play about a family leaving their home to claim land in Wapello County, Iowa.	props, costumes (optional)	1 session 50 min.	Lessons 1–4
Play: Moving West 👥👥 group Students perform a play about starting a new life in a new location.	props, costumes (optional)	1 session 50 min.	Lessons 1–4

Chapter **8** Short-Term Projects pages 84–85			
Fifteen Miles on the Erie Canal 👥👥 group Students sing or do a choral reading of the song, "The Erie Canal."	copies of song lyrics for "The Erie Canal"	1 session 30 min.	Lesson 1
Midwest Jigsaw Puzzle 👥 partners Students make puzzles from an outline map of the United States.	outline maps of the U.S., oaktag, paste, pencils, markers, scissors	1 session 30 min.	Lessons 1–3
More or Less? 👥 partners Students make diagrams explaining why parts of the Midwest are dry while others have more rain.	paper, pencils, crayons, markers, colored pencils	1 session 20 min.	Lessons 1–3
Erosion Demonstration 👥👥 group Students plan science fair projects demonstrating erosion.	paper, pencils, crayons or markers	1 session 20 min.	Lesson 2
A New Mt. Rushmore 👥👥 group Students discuss and nominate three recent figures to add to Mt. Rushmore.	paper, pencils, picture of Mt. Rushmore	1 session 20 min.	Lesson 2

Social Studies Plus!

Chapter 8 Writing Projects pages 86–87	Materials	⏰	Lesson Link
The Ocean Is . . . ♦ **individual** Students write descriptions of the ocean for someone who has never seen it.	paper, pencils	1 session 20 min.	Lesson 1
Transportation Charts ♦ **individual** Students create charts about the advantages and disadvantages of using barges, railroads, and trucks.	paper, pencils	1 session 20 min.	Lesson 1
Say It With Metaphors ♦ **individual** Students create their own metaphors.	paper, pencils	1 session 20 min.	Lessons 1–3
Made from Scratch ♦♦ **partners** Students make lists of things that we take for granted but that pioneers had to make "from scratch."	paper, pencils	1 session 25 min.	Lessons 1–3
Prairie Dogs ♦ **individual** Students write reports about prairie dogs.	paper, pencils	1 session 20 min.	Lesson 2
Chapter 8 Citizenship Project page 88			
Honesty ♦♦♦ **whole class** Students discuss the reasons that "honesty is the best policy."	paper, pencils	1 session 45 min.	Lessons 1–3
Chapter 9 Short-Term Projects pages 90–91			
Ojibwa Talking Stick ♦♦ **partners** Students make their own talking sticks.	construction paper, tape, crayons or markers, other materials	1 session 20 min.	Lesson 1
Floor Plan ♦♦ **partners** Students draw pictures of three different types of dwellings.	paper, pencils, crayons or markers	1 session 20 min.	Lessons 1–4
Work Songs ♦♦ **partners** Students create their own railroad, riverboat, or canal boat work songs.	paper, pencils, cassette tape and recorder	1 session 30 min.	Lessons 1–4
Midwest Mosts ♦♦♦ **group** Students plan and create exhibits titled "Midwest Mosts."	paper, pencils, crayons or markers, other materials as needed	1 session 20 min.	Lessons 1–4
Midwest Food Pyramid ♦ **individual** Students draw their own food pyramids.	construction paper, pencils	1 session 20 min.	Lessons 1–4
Pop! Pop! Pop! ♦♦ **partners** Students draw pictures with captions that show, step-by-step how a popcorn kernel pops.	encyclopedia and other research materials, paper, pencils, markers	1 session 20 min.	Lesson 3
Chapter 9 Writing Projects pages 92–93			
The Life of Sitting Bull ♦ **individual** Students write biographical sketches of Sitting Bull, the Lakota leader.	paper, pencils	1 session 20 min.	Lessons 1–2
Telling Tales ♦ **individual** Students write retellings of their favorite Native American tales.	paper, pencils	1 session 40 min.	Lessons 1–2

© Scott Foresman 4

Chapter **9** Writing Projects *continued*	Materials	🕐	Lesson Link
Causes and Effects 🧍 individual Students write cause-and-effect paragraphs explaining how the Europeans changed the lives of the Ojibwa.	paper, pencils	1 session 20 min.	Lessons 1–2
Best Way to Go 🧍 individual Students write their own advertisements persuading shippers to use a particular means of transportation.	paper, pencils	1 session 20 min.	Lessons 1–4
Midwest Menus 🧍 individual Students make their own restaurant menus including only foods that come from the Midwest.	paper, pencils	1 session 25 min.	Lessons 1–4
Life Stories 🧍 individual Students write autobiographical paragraphs describing a personal experience in a cherished activity.	paper, pencils	1 session 25 min.	Lessons 1–4
Chapter **9** Citizenship Project *page 94*			
Respect 🧍🧍🧍 whole class Students brainstorm a list of ways people can show respect for the environment	BLM p. 95, paper, pencils	1 session 40 min.	Lessons 1–4

Social Studies Plus!

NOTES

Long-Term Project

Midwest Market

So much of the food we eat comes from the Midwest, this region could be called our country's supermarket. Students will make a model supermarket stocked with Midwest goodies.

Brainstorming

Week 1

👨👧👦 whole class   🕐 15 minutes

Materials: none

• Get the class to brainstorm a list of foods we get from the Midwest. On the chalkboard list the items in categories—grains, fruits, meats, dairy products, for example. Here are some items students might think of: wheat, corn, soybeans, sunflowers, oats, barley, apples, cherries, peaches, plums, grapes, blueberries, strawberries, milk, cream, cheese, beef, pork, and lamb.

• Then discuss with the class the many specific food products that come from the foods students have mentioned. For example, flour, bread, and cereals come from wheat; applesauce and apple juice come from apples; ice cream, cheese, butter, and cream come from milk. Ask students where meat products come from (hogs, cattle, and sheep). Record the products on the chalkboard.

Planning

Week 2

👨👦 group   🕐 30–40 minutes

Materials: index cards, paper, pencils

• Write items from the class list on index cards—one item per card. Divide the class into groups. Have group members take turns picking cards from the pack until all the cards have been taken and all groups have approximately the same number of cards.

• The groups will create a model supermarket displaying food products of the Midwest. Students will design containers, packages, and labels for their products. Students should make a list of materials they will need as they plan. One member of each group should record the group's ideas. All group members should help collect materials.

© Scott Foresman 4

Stocking the Market

Weeks 3&4

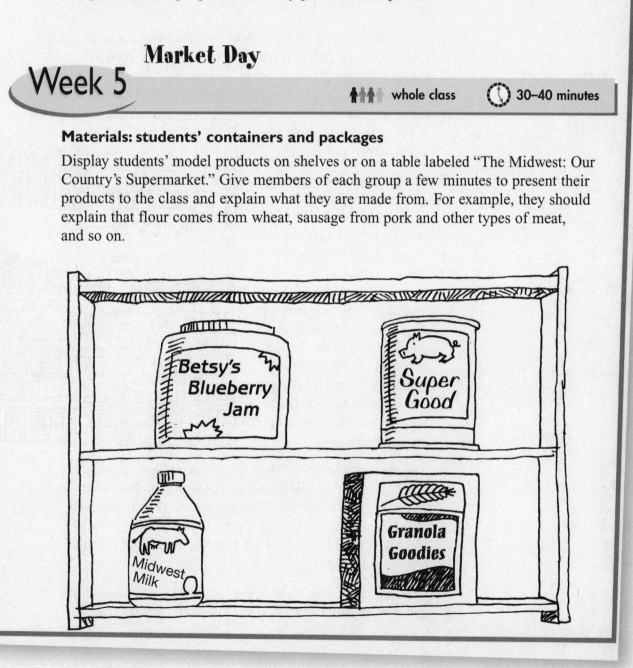

group   **20–30 minutes**

Materials: cardboard, boxes, bags, empty cans (cover edges with tape), plastic bottles and containers, modeling clay, plastic wrap, paper, crayons or markers, water, food coloring, scissors, tape

Working together in their group, students can now create packages and containers for the model supermarket. Encourage them to think creatively about how their products might be packaged and labeled. Remind students that packages and labels are designed to make people want to buy products in supermarkets.

Market Day

Week 5

whole class   **30–40 minutes**

Materials: students' containers and packages

Display students' model products on shelves or on a table labeled "The Midwest: Our Country's Supermarket." Give members of each group a few minutes to present their products to the class and explain what they are made from. For example, they should explain that flour comes from wheat, sausage from pork and other types of meat, and so on.

© Scott Foresman 4

Land Rush

Students improvise reactions to moving into new homes as a warm-up for a drama about people who found new lives in the Midwest during the 1843 land rush.

"Moving" Improvisation

Have students play the following improvisation game in a group:

1. The first student in the group to be "it" closes his or her eyes and visualizes that when he or she opens them a house will appear. The student will suppose that he or she is about to move into the house along with family members and that the house is far away from where the family lives now.

2. The other students in the group confer briefly to decide what kind of a house will appear—a castle, a mansion, a one-room log cabin, an apartment on an upper floor of a high-rise apartment building in a big city, a cozy cottage in the country, and so on. They will also tell the student where the house is located, making sure to choose a location far away from their present hometown.

3. The student who is "it" then opens his or her eyes and acts out exploring the new home, commenting on what he or she sees, likes or doesn't like, and so on. The student will also ask questions, voicing any worries or concerns he or she might have about moving away from familiar friends and surroundings.

4. Other students take turns being "it" until all students in the group have had a chance to explore their new homes.

Social Studies Plus!

Discussion

Have students meet in their group for fifteen or twenty minutes to discuss their improvisation experiences. On the chalkboard, write several discussion starters to help them begin:

1. How would you describe your reactions to your new home?

2. Which adjectives would you use to describe your feelings about moving to the new place—excited, worried, happy, sad, scared, curious?

3. In what ways did you think your life would change when you moved into the new home?

4. What are the pros and cons of living in the same place all the time?

5. What are the pros and cons of changing the place you live once in a while?

Let students know that they are not required to use the discussion questions on the board, but they may use them for help getting started if they're not sure what to talk about.

After students have completed their group discussions, bring the class together to talk about how the settlers who came to the Midwest in the early 1800s must have felt about moving. Get the discussion going by asking the following questions:

1. Where did the settlers come from?

2. What might have been their reasons for moving west?

3. How did they get to the Midwest? What do you imagine the journey was like?

4. What did they have to do when they reached their destination?

5. What were some of the difficulties they faced?

6. In what ways did their lives change?

Tell students they should continue to think about the questions they have been considering as they perform their roles in the drama *Moving West.*

Moving West

The year is 1843. A family is about to leave their home,
join the land rush, and claim land in Wapello County, Iowa.
What will their new lives be like?

Part 1: Ready, Set, Go!

The Parts: (6 players)
- Mother
- Elizabeth
- Joshua
- Father
- Alice
- Ben

Director's Notes: Some players will memorize their parts. Other players will improvise, or make up, their lines. With your group, brainstorm what players might say as they discuss their feelings about the new life they are about to begin. Remind players that the improvisations and discussions they have participated in should help them with their parts in the drama.

Tell your players to watch for stage directions in the play. They are shown in parentheses.

(Improv Directions: Players are sitting in the parlor, or living room, of their modest but comfortable rented house in the Northeast.)

Father: I hope you all have your things packed. Tomorrow morning, we'll be on our way to Iowa.

Ben: *(clapping his hands)* I can't wait!

Elizabeth: *(jumping up and down)* Neither can I. I've never been so excited in all my life!

Alice: I don't see why we have to go. What's wrong with staying here? *(Improv Directions: Talk about why she doesn't want to leave the family's home.)*

Joshua: I agree with Alice. Why are we going to Iowa, anyway? What will it be like when we get there?

Mother: *(smiling bravely)* It will be nice. *(Improv Directions: Talk about why the family is going to move.)* We'll be starting a whole new life.

Joshua: *(shrugging his shoulders)* I don't see what's wrong with the life we have here.

Elizabeth: I think it will be wonderful to have our own farm and a home we own ourselves.

Ben: I'm going to help Dad build our house. We're going to make it really nice.

Father: We'll make it as nice as we can. *(**Improv Directions:** Talk about what the house might be like.)*

Mother: Well, like it or not, our decision is made. We leave in the morning, so everybody get a good night's sleep.

Alice: *(looking around room)* Our last night at home.

Moving West

Starting a new life is exciting. But it isn't easy. There's plenty of work to be done before the cold winter sets in.

Part 2: A New Home

The Parts: (5–6 players—The same family as in Part 1, but acted by a different group of players)

Director's Notes: Some players will memorize their parts. Other players will improvise, or make up, their lines. With your group, brainstorm what players might say about their new life in a one-room sod house on the prairie.

Tell your players to watch for stage directions in the play. They are shown in parentheses.

(Players are standing outside their one-room sod hut, which has just been completed.)

Father: *(standing with arms folded)* Well, that's it. It's not much, but it should keep us warm when winter sets in.

Joshua: I guess it'll be better than living in the wagon.

Mother: We'll make the house as comfortable as we can. *(**Improv Directions:** Talks about how they will fix up the house to make it comfortable.)*

Elizabeth: It will be cozy all staying together in the same room.

Alice: Cozy and crowded.

Ben: We all worked hard on this house. I think we should be proud of it.

Father: Ben has the right idea. And we should be proud of our farm, too. Come the fall, we'll be harvesting our first crops.

Alice: I *am* proud. It's just that I still miss our own home. *(**Improv Directions:** Talks about what she misses about life back East.)*

Mother: *(holding up an imaginary piece of fabric)* Alice, will you help me make curtains for the windows of our house? I brought some pretty material with us for just that purpose.

© Scott Foresman 4

Alice: Of course I'll help, Mother. *(**Improv Directions:** Talks about how she's starting to feel better.)*

Joshua: What I can do to help?

Father: There's plenty for everyone to do here. If we work together, we'll have a good life.

Short-Term Projects

Hills, plains—rainy weather, dry weather—farms, cities—the Midwest has it all.
The following projects invite your students to explore this varied region.

Midwest Jigsaw Puzzle   👤 partners   🕐 30 minutes

Materials: outline maps of the United States, oaktag, paste or glue, pencils, crayons or markers, scissors

1. On an outline map of the United States, students draw a border around the Midwest and label each state. The maps on pages 234 and 247 of their textbooks will help them locate and identify states.

2. Students color the states of the Midwest, using two different colors for the Great Lakes states (Ohio, Michigan, Indiana, Illinois, Wisconsin, Minnesota) and the Central Plains states (Iowa, Missouri, North Dakota, South Dakota, Nebraska, Oklahoma, Kansas).

3. Students cut out the Midwestern states and paste them onto a sheet of oaktag. After cutting out each separate state, students will have a Midwest jigsaw puzzle to put together and with which to challenge other students.

A New Mt. Rushmore   👨‍👩‍👧 group   🕐 20 minutes

Materials: paper, pencils, picture of Mt. Rushmore

Mt. Rushmore in the Black Hills of South Dakota has been sculpted to represent four leaders of our country: George Washington, Thomas Jefferson, Abraham Lincoln, and Theodore Roosevelt. Invite groups to discuss and nominate three more recent figures in United States history to add to the mountain. List all nominations on the board and have the class vote for three additions to Mt. Rushmore. Suggest that nominees represent both women and minority groups as well as men. Students can draw pictures of the new Mt. Rushmore with the added figures.

More or Less?

Materials: paper, pencils, outline map of the United States

Invite students to make diagrams that explain why parts of the Midwest are dry, while other parts have more rain. On a map of the United States, students should outline the Midwestern region, indicating the location of the Rocky Mountains and the Gulf of Mexico. They can draw arrows to represent winds moving east over the Rocky Mountains and dotted lines to represent rain falling on the western slopes of the mountains. Students can draw arrows to represent winds moving north from the Gulf of Mexico and dotted lines to show rain falling on the states of the central and eastern plains.

Remember! Keep working on that Long-Term Project.

Erosion Demonstration

group **20 minutes**

Materials: paper, pencils, crayons or markers

Invite students to plan a possible science fair project demonstrating erosion by wind, rain, glaciers, or rivers. Group members can brainstorm what their proposed projects will demonstrate and how. Then they should do some research on erosion. An article in a good encyclopedia will give them the information they need. Students can draw the steps of the project, providing explanatory captions.

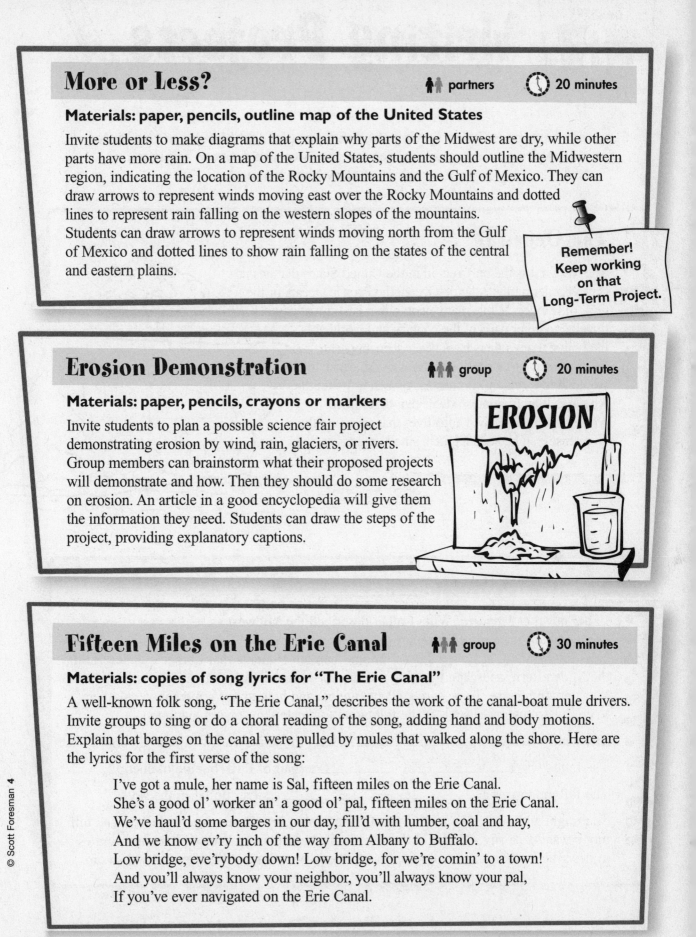

Fifteen Miles on the Erie Canal

group **30 minutes**

Materials: copies of song lyrics for "The Erie Canal"

A well-known folk song, "The Erie Canal," describes the work of the canal-boat mule drivers. Invite groups to sing or do a choral reading of the song, adding hand and body motions. Explain that barges on the canal were pulled by mules that walked along the shore. Here are the lyrics for the first verse of the song:

> I've got a mule, her name is Sal, fifteen miles on the Erie Canal.
> She's a good ol' worker an' a good ol' pal, fifteen miles on the Erie Canal.
> We've haul'd some barges in our day, fill'd with lumber, coal and hay,
> And we know ev'ry inch of the way from Albany to Buffalo.
> Low bridge, eve'rybody down! Low bridge, for we're comin' to a town!
> And you'll always know your neighbor, you'll always know your pal,
> If you've ever navigated on the Erie Canal.

Chapter 8 Writing Projects

Students have been investigating the land, people, and history of the Midwest. Here are some opportunities for them to use written expression to extend what they have learned.

The Ocean Is . . .

The Midwest is the only region in the United States that has no states bordering the Atlantic Ocean, the Pacific Ocean, or the Gulf of Mexico. While many people in the Midwest have traveled to other parts of the country and world, it is likely that many others have never seen an ocean. Invite students to write descriptions of the ocean that would help a person who has never seen it to imagine what it is like. Remind students that descriptive writing should use vivid adjectives that appeal to the five senses: sight, sound, touch, smell, and taste.

Say It with Metaphors

In her novel *O Pioneers!* Willa Cather described the Midwest as ". . . a vast checkerboard marked off in squares of wheat and corn . . ." Briefly discuss with the class the meaning of Cather's description. Then tell students that Cather was describing the Midwestern landscape by using a *metaphor*—describing something by saying that it is something else. To be sure students understand how to use a metaphor, ask them to complete sentences such as the following to create their own metaphors:

The wind was a _____ (howling wolf, whirling ghost).

The kitten was a _____ (ball of fluff, bundle of energy).

The full moon was a _____ (silver dollar in the sky).

You might add that a *simile* is similar to a metaphor but it uses the word *like*. (The full moon was *like* a silver dollar in the sky.) Invite students to use metaphors and similes to describe landscapes that are familiar to them: mountains, hills, forests, and so on.

Made from Scratch

Discuss with the class the self-sufficiency of the pioneers who settled in the Midwest. They were able to bring with them only a few possessions to help them begin their new lives. Just about everything they needed, they had to make themselves. Ask students to suggest what some of these things were (soap, furniture, clothing, and so on). Invite students to work in pairs to make lists of things that we take for granted but that pioneers had to make "from scratch." Suggest students get ideas by visualizing things around their own homes, including items in their refrigerators, drawers, and closets.

Prairie Dogs

Students have learned that one of the many kinds of animals that live on the prairie is the prairie dog. Invite students to research prairie dogs to find out why they are well adapted to their prairie habitat. Have students write brief illustrated reports about prairie dogs including information about their habits and habitat. A good encyclopedia should provide adequate information for student's reports.

Transportation Charts

Invite students to reread the section of their textbook that explains the advantages and disadvantages of using barges, railroads, and trucks for the transportation of different kinds of goods. Encourage them to compile the information they have learned into charts. The charts might list "barge," "railroad," and "truck" in the left-hand column. Other information could appear in two other columns headed "Advantages" and "Disadvantages."

Citizenship

Honesty

**Honesty is the best policy for many reasons.
One of those reasons is that honesty builds trust. And trust is a necessary
ingredient for good relationships with others.**

Discuss with students the reasons that "honesty is the best policy." Lead them to include as one of their reasons the fact that honesty builds trust. In other words, if people know that you are honest in most situations, they will show they trust you by believing what you say and having faith that you will keep your promises. As concrete examples, present the class with the following situations and ask students why they would or would not trust the person in each situation:

1. You have a part in a school play. Your friend comes to a rehearsal. Afterward, you ask him how he thought you did. You expect him to be polite and say "Great!" but instead he says that he thinks you should speak more loudly and with more expression in your voice.

2. You and a friend have agreed to go to a movie on Saturday afternoon. Your friend calls you on the phone Saturday morning and says she has to stay home because she is sick. Then you find out she went to the mall with another friend.

3. You go to a store with a friend. Your friend takes a candy bar, puts it in his pocket, and walks out without paying.

4. You invite a friend to come over to your house after school. She feels like staying home with her mom instead. She could make an excuse—saying she has too much homework, for example—but instead she tells you the truth.

After discussing which people students would or would not trust and why, talk about how the people in situations two and three could have acted differently and why students would be more likely to trust them if they had acted honestly.

© Scott Foresman 4

Social Studies Plus!

Good Advice

In each box, write the advice you would give a friend about how to act in the situation described.

My best friend asked me to go to the mall after school, but I don't feel like going. What should I say?

_____
_____
_____
_____

I forgot to do my math homework last night. What should I tell my teacher?

_____
_____
_____
_____

I have to write a book report. My sister has one that she wrote on the same book last year. Should I use my sister's report?

_____
_____
_____
_____

Short-Term Projects

Students have been introduced to the history, the people, and the products of the Midwest. Invite students to respond creatively to what they've been learning about this region.

Floor Plan

👫 partners   🕐 20 minutes

Materials: paper, pencils, crayons or markers

Students have learned that the pioneers who settled the Midwest built one-room log cabins or houses made of sod. Invite students to choose one of these types of dwellings and draw it. Their pictures should include a representation of the outside of the house and a floor plan of the inside, showing areas for sleeping, cooking, eating, and other activities.

Work Songs

👫 partners   🕐 30 minutes

Materials: paper, pencils, cassette tape and recorder (optional)

Students have learned that some people in the Midwest worked on railroads, riverboats, or canal boats. Explain that people often used to sing while working. Sing with the class "I've Been Working on the Railroad," "The Erie Canal," or another familiar work song. Invite students to work with partners to create their own railroad, riverboat, or canal boat work songs. They can use the melodies of folk songs they already know. Encourage partners to perform or record their songs for the class.

Midwest Mosts

group 👪   🕐 20 minutes

Materials: paper, pencils, crayons or markers, other materials as needed

Make students aware that the Midwest is a region of "mosts": Iowa grows the most corn of any state in the United States, Kansas grows the most wheat, and most breakfast cereals come from grains grown in the Midwest. Wisconsin produces the most milk and cheese, and most of our iron is produced in the Mesabi Range in Minnesota. O'Hare Airport in Chicago, Illinois, is the nation's busiest airport. Invite groups to plan and create exhibits titled "Midwest Mosts."

Ojibwa Talking Stick

👥 partners   🕐 20 minutes

Materials: large sheets of construction paper, tape, crayons or markers, other materials as needed

The Ojibwa used an object called a "talking stick" to make sure that only one person—the person holding the stick—talked at a time during council meetings. When that person passed the stick on, another person could speak. This practice kept their meetings organized and orderly. Invite students to make their own talking sticks out of rolled-up construction paper decorated any way they wish. They can use the talking sticks to pass around during class discussions.

Remember! Keep working on that Long-Term Project.

Pop! Pop! Pop!

👥 partners   🕐 20 minutes

Materials: encyclopedia and other research materials, paper, pencils, crayons or markers

Popcorn, a product that most students know and love, is a special kind of corn. And, like most corn, it is grown in the Midwest. How many students know what makes popcorn pop? Invite them to find out by doing research. They can probably find what they need to know from a good encyclopedia. Each popcorn kernel has a tiny bit of moisture inside. When the kernel is heated, the moisture turns into steam. The steam builds up inside the kernel until the kernel explodes. The explosion blows the kernel inside out! Have students draw pictures with captions that show, step-by-step, how a popcorn kernel pops.

Midwest Food Pyramid

🧍 individual   🕐 20 minutes

Materials: construction paper, pencils

The Food Guide Pyramid shows how to eat in a healthy way. It is a triangle with the bottom, or largest part, labeled "bread, cereal, rice, and pasta"; the second part from the bottom labeled "vegetables and fruits"; the third section labeled "meat and dairy products"; and the top, or smallest part, labeled, "fats and sweets." Invite students to draw their own food pyramids. They should leave enough room in each section of the pyramid to write in products that come from the Midwest.

Writing Projects

Invite students to express in writing what they have discovered about the contributions the Midwest makes to our country.

Best Way to Go

What's the best way to send goods from the Midwest to other parts of the country: barge, train, or truck? Have students choose one or more Midwestern products. Invite them to write their own print advertisements to persuade shippers to use one of these means of transportation. Suggest students consider products such as fresh fruits and vegetables, coal, metals, and meat. Ask them to consider speed, cost, delivery method, and capacity (how much a barge, truck, or freight car can hold) in deciding which method of shipping is best for each product.

Midwest Menus

So much of the food we eat comes from the Midwest! Invite students to make their own restaurant menus including only foods that come from this region. Encourage them to include as many different kinds of foods as possible. Suggest that, before students write, they hold brainstorming sessions to make lists of their favorite foods. Have students refer to the Food Guide Pyramid to categorize their foods.

The Life of Sitting Bull

Sitting Bull, the Lakota leader, is an important figure in Native American history. Invite students to research the life of Sitting Bull and to write brief biographical sketches of this great Native American leader. Suggest that students use encyclopedias or the Internet to find their information.

Telling Tales

Encourage students to visit the library to find Native American tales from Midwestern tribes—the Ojibwa, Sioux, Ottawa, and Potawatomi tribes. Invite students to read some of the tales they find and write their own retellings of one of their favorites. Remind students that in narrative writing, the writer should be careful to keep events in time order. Remind them, also, to make their tales as fun to read as possible by including dialogue and lots of action verbs.

Causes and Effects

Students have read about how, in the 1600s, the arrival of Europeans drastically changed the lives of the Ojibwa. Invite them to write cause-and-effect paragraphs explaining these changes and why they occurred. Remind students that a cause-and-effect paragraph tells what happened and explain what caused it to happen. Students should consider how the arrival of the Europeans affected the Ojibwa way of life (including the landscape and animal population of the Midwest).

Life Stories

Mark Twain's *Life on the Mississippi* captured the author's experiences as a trainee pilot on a Mississippi River steamboat and his love for life on the river. Is there some activity in students' lives that they really enjoy? Invite students to write an autobiographical paragraph that describes a personal experience in a cherished activity. Have them give a title to their work that is similar to Twain's, such as "Life at the Mall," "Life on the Team," or "Life on the Beach."

Citizenship

Respect

Respecting other people's feelings is important. So is respecting other people's rights. But there's another kind of respect that's important too—respect for the environment.

With the class, brainstorm what we mean by the word *respect*. Students will probably mention being polite to others, being careful not to hurt others' feelings, and not infringing on the rights of others. Lead students to understand that another kind of respect is respect for the environment. Ask them what they think respecting the environment means and why it is important. If people neglect to show respect for the environment, what will be the negative effects on our planet and our way of life?

Invite students to brainstorm a list of ways people can show respect for the environment. Their list might include the following:

• Don't throw litter on the ground.

• Pick up litter that you see on the ground and throw it in a trash basket.

• Recycle metal, plastic, and paper instead of throwing it in the trash.

Next, present students with the following situations and ask them to give examples of respectful behavior that people might exhibit in each situation:

• Hiking with a group in the woods

• Playing ball outside with friends

• Spending an evening at home

You might begin a chart on the chalkboard and fill it in as students give their examples.

Finally, ask students to suggest ways in which they can encourage others to respect the environment. What could they do to change the behavior of people who disrespect the environment in situations like the ones the class has discussed? Students' suggestions might include speaking to others, showing respectful behavior by example, putting up posters advertising respect for the environment, and writing concerned letters to a local newspaper.

Students can use the blackline master on page 95 to create bumper stickers for people to attach to their cars to advertise respect for the environment. Invite students to work in pairs or group to talk about clever bumper stickers they have seen and to brainstorm slogans or rhymes they could use for the bumper stickers they will create.

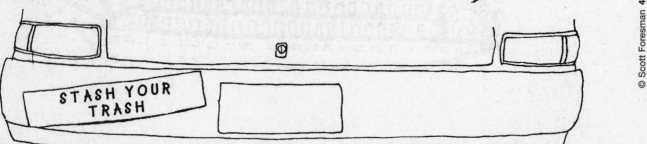

STASH YOUR TRASH

Bumper Sticker

Use this page to make your own bumper sticker encouraging people to have respect for the environment. One is done for you.

Stash Your Trash

Teacher Planner

Long-Term Project pages 98–99	Materials	🕐	Lesson Link
A Desert Mural Students explore the landforms, plants, and animals of the deserts of the Southwest by creating a mural.			Lessons 1–2
Week 1 👥 whole class Students brainstorm things to include in their murals.	none	1 session 15 min.	
Week 2 👥 group Students sketch notes on how plants and animals are adapted for desert living.	paper, pencils, research materials about the desert	1 session 40–45 min.	
Week 3 👥 group Students meet to share the information they have found.	paper, pencils	1 session 30 min.	
Week 4 👥 group Students draw their chosen images on the murals.	light blue paper, light brown paper, pencils, erasers, crayons, markers	1 session 1 hr.	
Week 5 👥 group Students identify the plants, animals, or landforms they have drawn on their murals.	completed mural	1 session 30 min.	
Unit Drama pages 100–105			
Play: The Grand Canyon 👥 group Students perform a play about experiencing the Grand Canyon.	props, costumes (optional)	1 session 40 min.	Lesson 1
Play: The Grand Canyon 👥 group Students perform a play about taking a mule trip down the Grand Canyon.	props, costumes (optional)	1 session 40 min.	Lesson 1
Play: The Grand Canyon 👥 group Students perform a play about the Colorado River in the Grand Canyon.	props, costumes (optional)	1 session 40 min.	Lesson 1
Chapter 10 Short-Term Projects pages 106–107			
Grand Canyon Model 👥 partners Students build models showing the physical characteristics of the Grand Canyon.	clay, clay-modeling tools, paper, markers*, tape	1 session 20 min.	Lesson 1
Places to Preserve 👥 group Students draw pictures of places they hope will be preserved for future generations.	paper, pencils, pictures from travel guides and magazines	1 session 20 min.	Lesson 1
Model Cliff Dwellings 👥 partners Students create models of Anasazi cliff dwellings.	clay, small cardboard boxes, clay-modeling tools, scissors, tape	1 session 30 min.	Lesson 1

* or crayons

Social Studies Plus!

Chapter 10 Short-Term Projects *continued*	Materials	🕐	Lesson Link
Hot Information 👥 partners Students choose a way to show average temperatures for specific places.	paper, graph paper, pencils, markers*	1 session 20 min.	Lessons 1–3
Desert Diorama 👥 partners Students make shoe box dioramas of desert scenes.	shoe boxes, sand, clay, oaktag, pencils, markers*, scissors, tape	1 session 30 min.	Lesson 2

Chapter 10 Writing Projects page108–109			
Grand Canyon Journal 👤 individual Students write journal entries that describe seeing the Grand Canyon for the first time.	paper, pencils	1 session 20 min.	Lesson 1
Explaining Erosion 👤 individual Students write explanations in their own words of how erosion contributed to the formation of the Grand Canyon.	paper, pencils	1 session 20 min.	Lesson 1
Crude Oil Chemistry 👤 individual Students research how products derived from crude oil are made.	paper, pencils	1 session 25 min.	Lesson 3
Origins of Oil 👤 individual Students write paragraphs explaining what they have found out about where oil comes from.	paper, pencils	1 session 20 min.	Lesson 3

Chapter 10 Citizenship Project page110			
Responsibility 👥👥 whole class Students talk about responsibilities that children their age might have.	BLM p. 111, paper, pencils	1 session 45 min.	Lessons 1–3

Chapter 11 Short-Term Projects pages 112–113			
Nature Posters 👤 individual Students design and draw posters titled "Southwest Wonders."	poster-sized paper, pencils, markers*	1 session 20 min.	Lesson 1
Navajo Crafts 👤 individual Students make their own jewelry or create blanket designs.	clay, clay-modeling tools, scraps of cloth, paints and brushes	1 session 30 min.	Lesson 1
Speaking of Spanish 👥 partners Students look up Spanish or Spanish-related words we use in English.	Spanish-English dictionaries	1 session 20 min.	Lesson 2
Let's Plan a Rodeo! 👥👥 group Students plan a class rodeo in which they can show off their own skills.	paper, pencils, crayons, markers	1 session 25–30 min.	Lesson 3
Song of the Southwest 👥👥 whole class Students learn the song "Red River Valley."	copies of song lyrics for "Red River Valley"	1 session 20 min.	Lesson 3
Booking the Southwest 👥 partners Students create a table of contents and an illustrated cover for possible books about modern life in the Southwest.	paper, markers*	1 session 15 min.	Lesson 4

* or crayons

Chapter 11 Writing Projects pages 114–115	Materials	🕐	Lesson Link
Diary of a Quest 👤 **individual** Students write diary entries about their quest for gold with Coronado in the year 1540.	paper, pencils	1 session 20 min.	Lesson 2
"Cinco de Mayo" Celebration 👤 **individual** Students write plans for their own *Cinco de Mayo* celebration that detail three different activities.	paper, pencils	1 session 25 min.	Lesson 2
On the Chisholm Trail 👤 **individual** Students write sets of written directions a person could use to travel the Chisholm trail.	paper, pencils	1 session 25 min.	Lesson 3
Make Yourself Comfortable 👤 **individual** Students think of inventions that would make people more comfortable in their region, and write descriptions of them.	paper, pencils	1 session 20 min.	Lesson 4

Chapter 11 Citizenship Project page 116			
Courage 👤👤👤 **whole class** Students discuss and role-play how a person could respond to different situations courageously.	BLM p. 117, paper, pencils	1 session 40 min.	Lesson 3

NOTES

_____

_____

_____

_____

_____

_____

_____

_____

_____

_____

_____

_____

_____

_____

_____

_____

_____

_____

Long-Term Project

A Desert Mural

The desert is dry, there's no denying. But it has its own unique beauty. Invite students to explore the landforms, plants, and animals of the deserts of the Southwest.

Getting Organized

Week 1

👤👤👤 whole class   🕐 15 minutes

Materials: none

Tell students that they are going to create a desert mural as you talk about what they know of the desert. Remind them that deserts can be beautiful and varied. Many plants and animals are all specially adapted for life in this hot, dry habitat. Tell students that the class will divide into six groups to work on different elements of the mural: landforms, plants, birds, mammals, insects, and reptiles.

Research

Week 2

👤👤👤 group   🕐 40–45 minutes

Materials: paper, pencils, research materials about the desert from the classroom or library

Assign each of the groups a desert category and have them prepare for its part of the mural by finding out the names of landforms, plants, birds, mammals, insects, or reptiles that are found in the deserts of the Southwest. Ask students to make and sketch notes on how plants and animals are adapted for desert living. Here are some starter ideas:

landforms: mountain, mesa, butte, plateau, dune

plants: Joshua tree, saguaro cactus, palo verde, prickly pear, barrel cactus, mesquite, primrose, poppy

mammals: pronghorn antelope, bighorn sheep, ground squirrel, kit fox, coatimundi, mountain lion, bobcat, kangaroo rat, jackrabbit, coyote, bat

insects: yucca moth, spider, scorpion, harvester ant, termite, painted lady, darkling beetle, tarantula

reptiles: Gila monster, rattlesnake, sidewinder, collared lizard, fringe-toed lizard, desert tortoise, gecko

birds: roadrunner, woodpecker, red-tailed hawk, cactus wren, elf owl, hummingbird

© Scott Foresman 4

Making Plans

Week 3

👫👤 group   🕐 30 minutes

Materials: paper, pencils

Have the groups meet to share the information they have found. At their meetings, students can decide which animals, plants, or landforms they will contribute to the mural and which individual student will draw each item. Every student should pick one or two items to draw.

Putting in the Pictures

Week 4

👫👤 group   🕐 60 minutes

Materials: light blue paper, light brown paper, pencils, erasers, crayons, colored markers

Prepare a bulletin board for the mural by stapling light blue paper across the top half (sky) and light brown paper across the bottom half (ground). Invite each group to draw its chosen images on the mural. Have the landforms group go first and then the plant group. The mammals group should go third, the reptiles group fourth, the birds group fifth, and the insects group sixth. Caution students to leave room for everyone's drawings.

Share the Mural

Week 5

👫👤 group   🕐 30 minutes

Materials: the completed mural

When the mural is complete, give each group a few minutes to identify the plants, animals, or landforms it has drawn and to share with the class any interesting facts its members have discovered about their parts of the mural, for example, how particular plants or animals are specially adapted to desert living or how particular landforms were formed.

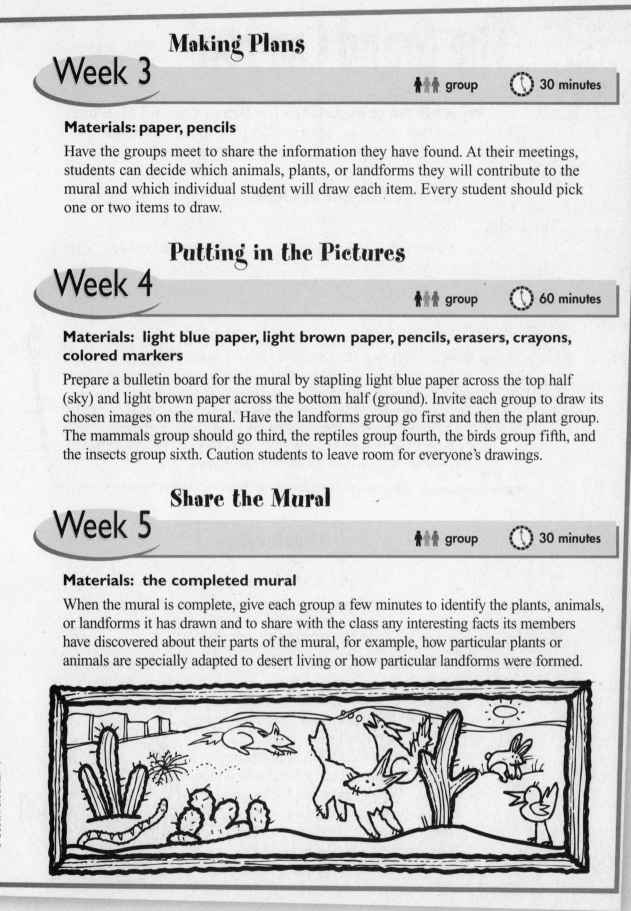

The Grand Canyon

What's it like to experience the Grand Canyon? Find out in this three-act play, as Captain Cárdenas finds something more precious than gold.

Act 1–A Canyon of Gold

The Parts:

(6 players)
- Narrator
- Soldier 1
- Soldier 3
- Capt. García de Cárdenas
- Soldier 2
- Soldier 4

Director's Notes: The narrator's part may be either memorized or read. Sometimes other players will improvise, or make up, their lines. With your group, brainstorm what players might say about seeing the Grand Canyon for the first time. Remind players that Cárdenas and his soldiers had no idea that such a place existed. Even though the soldiers were men, the players may be male or female. Tell your players to watch for stage directions in the play. They are given in parentheses.

Theater Talk

act: one of the main divisions of a play

lines: parts of the dialogue spoken by specific players

Narrator:

In the year 1540, Francisco Vásquez de Coronado, a Spanish explorer, was sent on a mission to search the lands north of Mexico. Coronado's orders were to find Cíbola, the Cities of Gold. As he explored the Southwest, he heard tales of a river that ran through a canyon of gold. He sent Capt. García López de Cárdenas and twelve soldiers to find that canyon. We now take you back more than 450 years to what is now the state of Arizona. Here come Capt. Cárdenas and some of his soldiers now. *(Enter Captain Cárdenas and four soldiers.)*

© Scott Foresman 4

Capt. Cárdenas: *(standing at the rim of the Grand Canyon with the others some distance behind him)* Stop!

Soldier 1: What does he see? Is it the canyon of gold? Was Coronado right?

Soldier 2: Are the stories really true? If they are, we'll all be rich!

Soldier 3: I must see this for myself. *(Shouts so that Cárdenas can hear.)* What do you see, Captain? Is it the canyon?

Soldier 4: *(also shouting)* May we come now, Captain?

Capt. Cárdenas: *(calling to his soldiers)* Come slowly. There is a canyon. I don't know what it is made of, but I have never seen anything like it!

(Soldiers catch up to Cárdenas. When they reach the canyon, the sight amazes them.)

Soldier 1: I have never seen anything so beautiful! *(Improv Directions: talks about the beauty of the canyon.)*

Soldier 2: I have never seen a canyon this deep or this wide. *(Improv Directions: talks about how huge the canyon is.)*

Soldier 3: Look at the river below! *(Improv Directions: talks about how the Colorado River looks from the rim of the canyon.)*

Soldier 4: I wonder if anyone has explored this place before. *(Improv Directions: talks about how they might get down the canyon and back up its walls.)*

Capt. Cárdenas: But is there gold in this canyon or not? *(Kneels down on the ground to look over the rim of the canyon and inspect its walls more closely.)* I do not think so. *(Improv Directions: talks about how they feel regarding the discovery of the canyon and the fact that its walls are not made of gold.)* Well, men, let's see what we can see. *(All exit.)*

The Grand Canyon

**Did you know that people can take trips
from the top of the Grand Canyon, down to its floor,
and back up again? How do they do it? By mule!**

Act 2–Canyon by Mule

The Parts: (6 players)
- Leader
- Student 1
- Student 2
- Student 3
- Student 4
- Student 5

Director's Notes: This part of the play features a group of students and their leader on a mule trip into the Grand Canyon. They began at the canyon's north rim and are on their way to the canyon floor. You might have players sit in chairs and pretend that they are riding mules.

Some players will memorize their parts. Some will also improvise, or make up, their lines. With your group, brainstorm what players might say about what they see and feel as they explore the canyon. You may also want to act as a prompter during the play to help players with their lines.

Theater Talk

prompter: person who whispers lines to players who have forgotten them

Leader: Everyone go slowly now! We're coming to a very steep part of the trail.

Student 1: *(to Student 2)* I wonder if this was a good idea? Maybe I should have gone to computer camp instead. *(**Improv Directions:** talks about fears and worries.)*

Student 2: I hear this canyon is about six thousand feet deep!

Student 3: Yeah, that's the height of seventeen Statues of Liberty or five Sears Towers!

Leader: Don't worry. Remember, we're on mules. Walking down a steep trail is a lot easier if you have four legs!

© Scott Foresman 4

Student 4: Right, I'm depending on old Sally here. I know she can make it!

Student 5: Stop worrying about the trail. Look around you! This place is amazing! *(Improv Directions: talks about the beauty and size of the canyon.)*

Leader: Yes, the canyon is about 277 miles long. It's 18 miles wide at its widest point.

Student 1: I've seen pictures of this place, but there's nothing like actually being here! *(Improv Directions: talks about feelings he or she had at first sight of the canyon.)*

Leader: Imagine how Captain Cárdenas and his soldiers must have felt the first time they came here. They didn't even know it existed!

Student 2: Yeah, but all they cared about was finding gold.

Student 3: Other people have looked for valuable metals here, too. Miners used to come here looking for zinc, copper, and lead.

Student 4: But it was too steep for mining, so they made money by charging people for trips through the canyon.

Student 5: I'm glad there are still trips into the canyon. This is really exciting!

Leader: We're coming to a flat place. We'll make camp here for the night.

Student 1: Well, we made it down after all!

Student 2: And I'm hungry. I can't wait to cook over the campfire.

Student 3: *(Improv Directions: talks about the day on the trail.)*

Student 4: I'm glad we're stopping here. I'm really tired, even though Sally here did all the work! *(Pats the mule on its "head.")*

© Scott Foresman 4

The Grand Canyon

Another way to see the Grand Canyon is from the bottom—on the Colorado River. Take an exciting raft trip through the canyon. Look up for an impressive sight!

Act 3–Down the River

The Parts:

(6 players)
- Leader
- Student 2
- Student 4

- Student 1
- Student 3
- Student 5

Director's Notes: In this part of the play, a group of students and their leader take a raft trip on the Colorado River through the Grand Canyon. You may want to have players sit on the floor and use cardboard oars as props for their roles.

Some players will memorize their parts. Some will also improvise, or make up, their lines. With your group, go over the script and brainstorm with players how they might react to the sights they see and the experience of rafting down the river and over rapids.

Theater Talk

prop: something other than painted scenes or costumes that is used in a play; short for "property"

Leader: Congratulations! You just went over your first rapids. Well done, group!

Student 1: Wow! That was fun!

Student 2: Yeah. And a little scary.

Student 3: I love riding the rapids! It's so exciting!

Student 4: What causes rapids, anyway?

Leader: The river bottom is rocky in some places. Where the water goes over a rock, it's like a tiny waterfall. If there are a lot of rocks, there are a lot of tiny waterfalls, one after the other. And if the river is moving fast, the water gets rough. That's why these rough areas are called rapids. *Rapid* means "fast."

Student 5:	We got soaking wet, but it feels good to me.
Student 1:	Yeah, I know what you mean. It's pretty hot down here, and the spray cools you off.
Leader:	The temperature is probably in the nineties down here, but up at the top of the canyon, it's much colder. Maybe in the sixties! You'd need jackets if you were up there now.
Student 2:	I can hardly see up to the top of the canyon. It looks even taller from down here than it did from the top. *(Improv Directions: talks about what it's like to look up the canyon walls.)*
Student 3:	We learned in school that Major John Wesley Powell made a boat trip through the Grand Canyon in 1869. He was the one who really got people interested.
Student 4:	Wasn't it Powell who named it the Grand Canyon in the first place?
Student 5:	I think so. And then Theodore Roosevelt worked to protect the canyon.
Student 1:	He said, "it's the one great sight which every American should see." *(Improv Directions: talks about why he or she agrees with Roosevelt.)*
Student 2:	The Grand Canyon became a national monument and then a national park. So people can't mine here anymore. And they can't cut down the trees for lumber. *(Improv Directions: talks about protecting beautiful places in our country and why it's important.)*
Student 3:	Isn't the U.S.A. great? We have so many beautiful places! *(Improv Directions: talks about other beautiful places in the United States.)*
Leader:	You all know a lot about the Grand Canyon. But I have one question for you.
Student 4:	What?
Leader:	Are you ready for more rapids?
Students:	*(shouting together)* Ready!
Leader:	Okay, here we go!

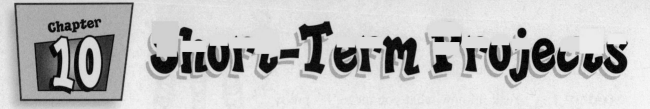

Short-Term Projects

Beautiful sunsets, dramatic landforms, Native American history and culture—
all this and more await visitors to the Southwest.
Invite your students to "visit" the Southwest creatively.

Grand Canyon Model

👫 partners   🕐 20 minutes

Materials: clay, clay-modeling tools, paper, crayons or markers, tape

Direct students to pictures of the Grand Canyon in the textbook. Suggest that partners talk about the physical characteristics of the Grand Canyon—its width, its depth, the appearance of its walls, and the width and color of the Colorado River at the canyon's base. Partners can plan how they will build models of the Grand Canyon with available materials and tools. Students then build their models and display them in the classroom.

Desert Diorama

👫 partners   🕐 30 minutes

Materials: shoe boxes, sand, clay, oaktag, pencils, crayons or colored markers, scissors, tape

Suggest that student partners revisit descriptions of the Southwest deserts in their textbook. Have them study pictures of the saguaro cactus, and desert animals such as the roadrunner, elf owl, kangaroo rat, and coyote. Invite students to make shoe box dioramas of desert scenes, including a saguaro cactus and several animals. Students may draw animals on oak tag, color, and cut them out. They may use clay for the cacti.

© Scott Foresman 4

Places to Preserve

👥 group   🕐 20 minutes

Materials: paper, pencils, pictures from travel guides and magazines that feature natural wonders such as national parks

Theodore Roosevelt once said of the Grand Canyon, "Do nothing to mar its grandeur. . . keep it for your children, your children's children, and all who come after you as the one great sight which every American should see." Invite students to meet in groups to brainstorm natural places they have seen, heard, or read about that they hope will be preserved for future generations to enjoy. Then they can draw pictures of places they have talked about. Each group can exhibit its pictures on a bulletin board "art gallery" titled "America the Beautiful."

Model Cliff Dwellings

👤 partners   🕐 30 minutes

Materials: clay, small cardboard boxes, clay-modeling tools, scissors, tape

Invite students to revisit photographs of Anasazi cliff dwellings. Encourage them to brainstorm in partners how to use a combination of clay and cardboard boxes to make models of the cliff dwellings. Have students work with their partners to create their models. Then they can compare and contrast their building methods with other students.

Remember! Keep working on that Long-Term Project.

Hot Information

👥 partners   🕐 20 minutes

Materials: paper, graph paper, pencils, crayons or markers

Have students study the map on page 309 of their textbook that compares average temperatures in different parts of the Southwest. Encourage partners to brainstorm other ways the same information could be presented—verbally, on a bar graph, or on a chart, for example. Challenge partners to choose a way to show average temperatures for several specific places, such as Austin, Texas; Yuma, Arizona; or Santa Fe, New Mexico.

Writing Projects

Students have been investigating the land and products of the Southwest. Through written expression, they can communicate their thoughts and ideas about what they have learned.

Grand Canyon Journal

Introduce this writing activity by telling students that most people who see the Grand Canyon for the first time are astonished at its vastness and profoundly moved by its great beauty. No matter what they have heard about the Grand Canyon and no matter how many times they have seen it in pictures, on television, or even on big movie screens, they are still stunned by their first sight of it.

Invite students to visualize they are seeing the Grand Canyon for the first time. Have them write journal pages describing what they see and their reactions to it. Suggest they use pictures of the Grand Canyon in the textbook for inspiration. Remind students that vivid, specific adjectives improve descriptive writing. They may want to make a list of their adjectives and write more vivid synonyms to use in a revision of their journal entry.

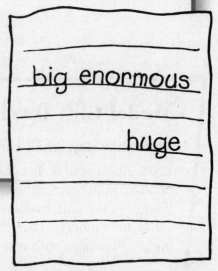

Explaining Erosion

Students have learned that scientists believe erosion played a part in forming the Grand Canyon. The rushing waters of the Colorado River, rain, glaciers, and sand and gravel carried by water and wind gradually wore away rock and soil, forming the Grand Canyon over thousands of years. Suggest that students reread the discussion of erosion on page 301 of the textbook. Invite them to write explanations in their own words of how erosion contributed to the formation of the Grand Canyon. Explain that this writing activity is good practice in **paraphrasing**—using one's **own words** to explain information from a passage that someone else has written. Remind them that paraphrasing is an important skill when writing research reports.

Crude Oil Chemistry

Students have learned that the Southwest—especially the state of Texas—provides much of our nation's oil. Direct students to the chart on page 315 of the textbook, which shows products made from the chemicals that come from crude oil.

Invite students to do further research about how one of these products is made. They could start by looking up *gasoline, detergent,* or *asphalt* in a good encyclopedia. They could also use an encyclopedia to look up specific kinds of fibers, such as nylon and polyester, used in clothing. They should take notes on the information they find.

When students write up the results of their research, they will be explaining steps in a process. Remind them to keep their writing in chronological order and to write very clearly so that readers will easily understand their explanations.

Origins of Oil

Students have learned that oil is a nonrenewable resource—one that cannot be replaced by nature. In addition, they know that oil is very important to our survival, since we depend on it for such necessities as heat and transportation. Invite students to do research to find out where oil comes from and how it is formed. They could start by looking up *oil* and *petroleum* in a good encyclopedia and then use several other books from the library, if necessary. Have them write two short paragraphs explaining what they have found out about where oil comes from. Their paragraphs should contain explanations for why oil is considered to be nonrenewable.

Citizenship

Responsibility

"I can count on you." Most of us take those words as a compliment. These activities help students consider how they can live up to the faith others have in them.

Invite students to talk about responsibilities that children their age might have. They may mention chores that children are responsible for at home, work they are responsible for at school, and things they are expected to do for friends and family members. You may also mention that people have responsibilities to themselves—to take care of their health and safety, for example. On the chalkboard, list the responsibilities that students mention under these categories: to family, to teachers, to friends, and to self.

Continue the discussion by suggesting situations that call for responsible action. For each situation, ask students to describe what they think that action would be.

1. Your parents are working on house repairs and painting. You are in charge of taking care of your two younger sisters or brothers for the afternoon. A friend calls and asks if you can go swimming. (Explain to the friend that you have promised to baby-sit today.)

2. Your friend is sick and will be out of school all week. He or she is worried about getting behind in schoolwork and homework. (Offer to call your friend about homework assignments.)

3. You walk home from school every day with the same group of friends. Often, you stop at a store to buy drinks or snacks to have on the way home. Some of the kids in your group are in the habit of throwing their drink containers or snack wrappers on the ground. (Say that you think it's irresponsible to throw trash on the ground. Or quietly pick up the trash and put it in a litter basket.)

4. On a winter day, you go to a nearby pond with two friends to go ice-skating. There is a warning sign next to the pond that says the ice is dangerous—it is too thin to skate on safely. Your friends say they're going to skate anyway. They tease you for being scared. (Take care of your own safety. Also strongly advise your friends not to skate. If they do anyway, notify a responsible adult.)

Invite students to fill in the speech balloons on the blackline master on page 111 with what they would say in the above situations.

THIN ICE NO SKATING

© Scott Foresman 4

Do the Right Thing

Fill in the blanks with the words you might say in each situation.

Your friend asks you to go swimming. You promised to baby-sit your sister today.

_____
_____
_____

Your sick friend needs books and homework assignments.

_____
_____
_____

Your friends are littering on the way home from school.

_____
_____
_____

Your friends want to ice-skate, but the sign reads Danger: No Skating!

_____
_____
_____

Short-Term Projects

The Southwest of yesterday still strongly affects the Southwest of today.
The following projects invite students to link Navajo, Spanish,
and cowboy cultures to modern life in the Southwest.

Nature Posters

individual   **20 minutes**

Materials: poster-sized paper, pencils, crayons or markers

Students have learned that an important part of Navajo culture is respect for nature. Invite students to brainstorm ideas for posters that would encourage people to respect the natural beauty and wonders of the Southwest. Have each student design and draw his or her own poster titled "Southwest Wonders." Display the posters in the classroom or around the school.

Navajo Crafts

individual   **30 minutes**

Materials: clay, clay-modeling tools, scraps of cloth, paints and paintbrushes or food coloring

Direct students to the photographs of Navajo jewelry and Navajo blanket. Invite them to make their own jewelry out of clay or to create their own blanket designs. Students choosing the jewelry project may want to simulate Navajo jewelry by using the colors of silver and turquoise. Students choosing the blanket-design project may want to simulate Navajo blankets by using geometric designs and earth tones as they paint on cloth.

Let's Plan a Rodeo!

group   **25–30 minutes**

Materials: paper, pencils, crayons, markers

At rodeos and Wild West shows in the Southwest, cowboys and cowgirls showed off their skills at riding, roping, and shooting. Rodeos are still held in the Southwest today. Invite groups of students to plan a class rodeo in which class members can show off their own skills—gymnastics, throwing and catching, running, or shooting baskets, for example. Students should list the events their "rodeos" would include and then create illustrated programs for spectators.

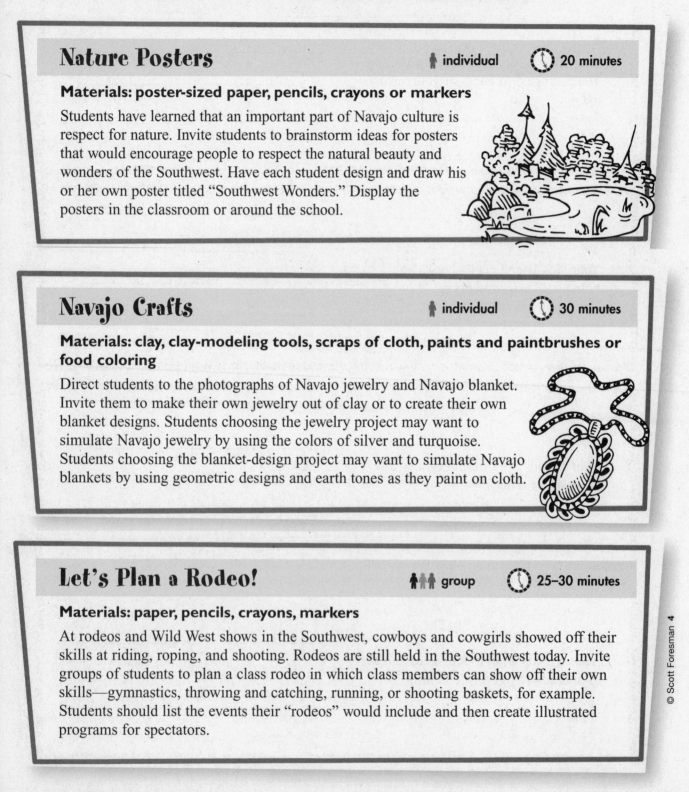

© Scott Foresman 4

Booking the Southwest

partners | **15 minutes**

Materials: paper, crayons or markers

Encourage students to review what they have learned about living in the Southwest today. Invite partners to discuss what topics they would cover if they were writing a book about modern life in the Southwest. Have partners create a table of contents, and an illustrated cover for their books.

Remember! Keep working on that Long-Term Project.

Song of the Southwest

whole class | **20 minutes**

Materials: copies of song lyrics

Give students copies of song lyrics for "Red River Valley"—a favorite cowboy love song. Tell students that the Red River runs through the Southwest of Texas and Oklahoma. Then invite students to learn the song or give choral readings of the lyrics.

Red River Valley

From this valley they say you are going,
We will miss your bright eyes and sweet smile,
For they say you are taking the sunshine,
That brightens our pathway a while.
Come and sit by my side if you love me,
Do not hasten to bid me adieu,
But remember the Red River Valley
And the girl that has loved you so true.

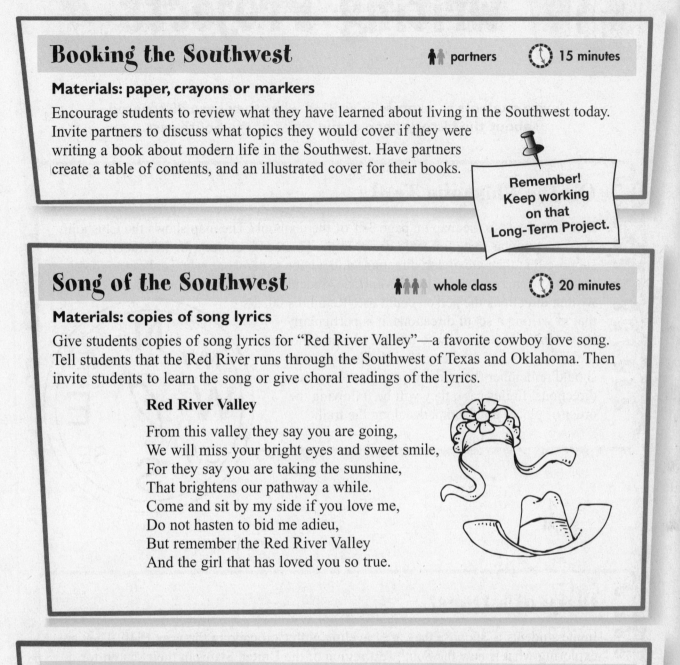

Speaking of Spanish

partners | **20 minutes**

Materials: Spanish-English dictionaries

Students have learned that the words *corral* and *rancho* have found their way into English through the Spanish and Mexican influence in the Southwest. Invite partners to take turns using a Spanish-English dictionary to look up additional Spanish or spanish-related words we use in English. Here are some suggestions: *rodeo* (corral, roundup), *mucho* (much), *patio* (courtyard), *brillo* (bright, sparkling), *bronco* (wild, untamed), *aventura* (adventure, danger), *cargo* (burden), *jaguar* (jaguar), *barrio* (neighborhood), *fiesta* (feast, festival), *siesta* (nap), *burro* (donkey), *calico* (cotton cloth), *padre* (father). Partners should make a chart showing the words they've looked up, their meanings, and their English equivalents.

Writing Projects

Invite students to express in writing what they have discovered
about the history, people, and cities of the Southwest.

On the Chisholm Trail

Direct students to the map on page 341 of the textbook. The map shows the Chisholm
Trail—a popular route for cattle drives in the nineteenth century. Invite students to
suppose that they are giving directions and advice to someone who is about to travel
the Chisholm Trail on a cattle drive. Have students use the map to create a set of
written directions the person could use. Remind students
that in writing a set of directions, it is particularly
important to write clearly so that the person following
the directions will not be confused. Also, students
should remember that order is important in writing
directions. In this case, they will be following the
order of places and landmarks along the trail.

Diary of a Quest

Invite students to suppose they are traveling with Coronado in the year 1540. They are
exploring what is now the Southwest region of the United States in their search for
gold. They have heard stories of magnificent cities made of gold and are hoping to
find them. Have students write diary entries about their quest for gold and their hopes,
fears, and expectations. Remind students that they do not have to stick to facts that
they have learned. Rather, they should be creative in writing their diary entries.

"Cinco de Mayo" Celebration

The Mexican holiday *Cinco de Mayo* (Fifth of May) celebrates a Mexican victory against French forces at Puebla, Mexico, in 1862. To give students an idea of the festive atmosphere of this holiday, direct them to the photograph of the twirling dancer at a *Cinco de Mayo* celebration on page 336 of the textbook. Encourage students to do further research about this holiday and how it is celebrated (food, dancing, games, and other activities that characterize the festival).

Have students write plans for their own *Cinco de Mayo* celebration that detail three different activities. Students' plans should be based on their research, but can also include original party activities they come up with themselves.

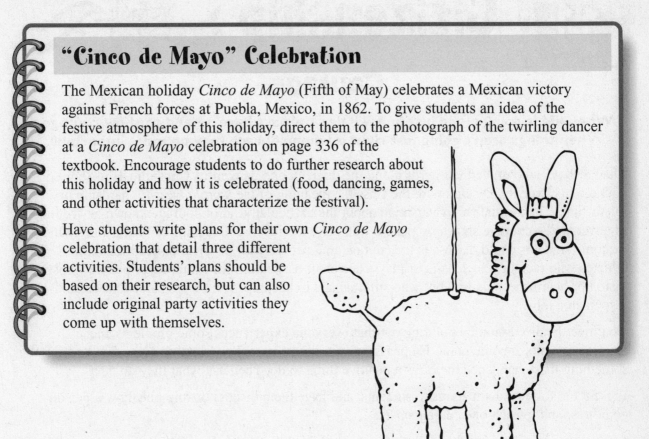

Make Yourself Comfortable

Students have learned about Willis Haviland Carrier and his work on the development of air-conditioning—an invention that makes almost all of us happier when the weather gets too hot for comfort. The air-conditioning system that Carrier helped develop made it possible for the Southwest—a region that is often uncomfortably hot—able to thrive and grow.

Challenge students to think of inventions that would make people more comfortable in your region. For example, if you live in an area that is often uncomfortably cold, a student may come up with a way to prevent people from getting cold when walking from the doors of their homes to their cars. Inventions can also relate to travel, noise control, pollution control, crowded conditions, and so on. For example, a student could come up with a way to get out of a traffic jam or a way for people to commute from their homes to work more efficiently. Have students write descriptions of their inventions and, if they wish, accompany their descriptions with illustrations.

Citizenship

Courage

When life is going along just fine, we don't always have a need to show courage. When things aren't going just right is when courage may be most important.

The cowboys who drove their herds along the difficult and dangerous Chisholm Trail showed courage in adversity. Discuss with the class the meaning of the word *adversity:* hardship or misfortune. Then initiate a conversation about the particular kind of courage known as "courage in adversity"—courage shown by people who are experiencing hardships or misfortunes. One example students could discuss is the courage that people with physical disabilities show— athletes who race in wheelchairs or play wheelchair basketball, for example, or people whose vision or hearing is impaired but who still manage to keep up with their schoolwork or hold responsible jobs.

Continue the discussion by pointing out that everyone experiences some problems and disappointments at some point. Emphasize that telling a parent or friend that you feel bad about something that's happened to you is a positive thing to do. Then ask what they do next.

Present the following situations to students, and have them discuss or role-play how a person could respond to each one courageously:

1. You have been looking forward to your friend's birthday party. Everyone at the party will be going to the beach for the day. The morning of the party, you wake up with a sore throat and a fever. You know you're too sick to go.

2. You have a big part in a school play. Just before the performance, you start getting nervous. You get so nervous that when the curtain opens you can't remember your lines. The whole audience is waiting for you to begin.

3. You've moved from a small town to a big city. It's the first day at your new school. Some of the kids treat you like "the new kid." They don't make you feel welcome or try to be friends. You overhear someone make fun of you because you grew up in a small town. You feel different and left out.

As a wrap-up activity, ask students to give examples of people through history who showed courage when they were having difficulties. They may use the blackline master chart on page 117. Students may choose either famous people such as Rosa Parks or anonymous people such as flood victims.

© Scott Foresman 4

Characters with Courage

Have you heard of or read about people who show courage—even when things don't go their way? Fill in the chart to write about three of these people.

Person	Problem He or She Faced	How He or She Showed Courage
_____	_____	_____
	_____	_____
	_____	_____
	_____	_____
	_____	_____
_____	_____	_____
	_____	_____
	_____	_____
	_____	_____
	_____	_____
_____	_____	_____
	_____	_____
	_____	_____
	_____	_____

Unit 6 Teacher Planner

Long-Term Project pages 120–121	Materials	🕐	Lesson Link
Song of the West Students celebrate the Western regions of the United States with an original song.			Lessons 1–3
Week 1 🏃🏃🏃 whole class Students brainstorm tunes they already know.	chalkboard	1 session 15 min.	
Week 2 🏃🏃 group Students write verses for a class song called "Song of the West."	note cards, pencils	1 session 20 min.	
Week 3 🏃🏃 group Students copy all of the verses onto one lyric sheet.	paper, pencils	1 session 45 min.	
Week 4 🏃🏃 group Students each get copies of their song, and then sing it to the class.	copies of "Song of the West"	1 session 20 min.	

Unit Drama pages 122–127

	Materials	🕐	Lesson Link
Play: Shooting the West 🏃🏃 group Students perform a play about a documentary on the West.	props, costumes (optional)	1 session 40 min.	Lessons 1–3
Play: Scenes from the Past 🏃🏃 group Students perform a play about scenes from the history of the West.	props, costumes (optional)	1 session 40 min.	Lessons 1–3
Play: Let's Talk West 🏃🏃 group Students perform a play about interviewing characters from the West.	props, costumes (optional)	1 session 40 min.	Lessons 1–3

Chapter 12 Short-Term Projects pages 128–129

	Materials	🕐	Lesson Link
Rocky Mountain Field Guide 🏃🏃 group Students choose animals to research, draw, and write about.	paper, pencils, crayons or markers, research material about animals	1 session 45 min.	Lesson 1
Model Mountains 🏃🏃 group Students make their own model mountains out of clay.	cardboard, clay	1 session 30 min.	Lessons 1–2
Midwest Art Gallery 🏃 individual Students draw or paint pictures of topics on the West they have chosen.	paper, crayons, markers or paints and brushes	1 session 20 min.	Lessons 1–3
Product Maps 🏃🏃 partners Students make product maps of the states of the West.	paper, pencils, BLM p. 139	1 session 30 min.	Lessons 1–3
Tundra Dioramas 🏃🏃 partners Students create dioramas of the Alaskan tundra.	paper, pencils, crayons or markers, shoeboxes, tape, scissors	2 sessions 20 min.	Lesson 2

Social Studies Plus!

Chapter 12 Writing Projects pages 130–131	Materials	🕐	Lesson Link
Yellowstone Journal 👤 individual Students write journal entries about spending a day in Yellowstone Park.	paper, pencils	1 session 20 min.	Lesson 1
Portrait of the Sierra Nevadas 👤 individual Students write descriptions of the scene in the painting *Among the Sierra Nevada Mountains, California.*	paper, pencils	1 session 20 min.	Lesson 1
Mountain Haiku 👤 individual Students write their own haikus using photographs of western mountains for inspiration.	paper, pencils	1 session 25 min.	Lessons 1–2
Western Cookery 👤 individual Students write recipes for one or more dishes made with products of the West.	paper, pencils	1 session 25 min.	Lessons 1–3
What Makes a Volcano Erupt? 👤 individual Students write cause-and-effect paragraphs in their own words that explain this natural phenomenon.	paper, pencils	1 session 20 min.	Lesson 2
North and South: Compare and Contrast 👤 individual Students write paragraphs comparing the climates in the northern and southern parts of California.	paper, pencils	1 session 20 min.	Lesson 3

Chapter 12 Citizenship Project page 132

Caring 👥👥 whole class Students discuss the importance of caring about others.	BLM p. 133, paper, pencils	1 session 45 min.	Lessons 1–3

Chapter 13 Short-Term Projects pages 134–135

Totem Pole Stories 👤 individual Students present designs to the class, explaining how the images relate to their characters' stories.	paper, pencils, crayons or markers	1 session 20 min.	Lesson 1
Beautiful Blankets 👤 individual Students make designs for their own blankets.	paper, pencils, crayons or markers	1 session 20 min.	Lesson 1
History Time Lines 👥 partners Students make time lines showing the history of the West.	paper, pencils, tape	1 session 20 min.	Lessons 2–3
Songs of the Cowboys 👥👥 group Students sing well-known folk songs about cowboys.	copies of song lyrics	1 session 30 min.	Lesson 2
"Go West" Bumper Stickers 👥 partners Students make bumper stickers to let people know of the West's many opportunities for recreation.	paper, pencils, crayons, markers	1 session 20 min.	Lesson 2
Filling Needs 👥👥 group Students invent products to fill today's needs.	paper, pencils	1 session 20 min.	Lesson 2

Chapter **13** **Writing Projects** pages 136–137	**Materials**	🕐	**Lesson Link**
Plan a Potlatch Party 🚶 individual Students write plans for a potlatch-style class party.	paper, pencils	1 session 30 min.	Lesson 1
Compare and Contrast Cities 🚶 individual Students write paragraphs comparing two cities studied in the chapter.	paper, pencils	1 session 20 min.	Lessons 1–3
Tell a Tall Tale 🚶 individual Students make up their own original Wild West tales with cowboy heroes of their own creation.	paper, pencils	1 session 25 min.	Lesson 2
Wild West Mayor 🚶 individual Students write campaign speeches in which the candidate tells the voters what he or she will do to bring law and order to the town.	paper, pencils	1 session 20 min.	Lesson 2
Gold Rush Skits 🚶 individual Students write their own skits in which the characters are involved in the Gold Rush.	paper, pencils	1 session 30 min.	Lesson 2
Messages from L.A. 🚶 individual Students write postcards or e-mail messages telling what they are doing on vacation in L.A.	paper, pencils	1 session 20 min.	Lesson 2
Chapter **13** **Citizenship Project** page 138			
Fairness 🚶🚶🚶 whole class Students decide why different situations are fair or unfair.	paper, pencils	1 session 40 min.	Lessons 1–3

Social Studies Plus!

NOTES

Long-Term Project

Song of the West

Varied and beautiful landscapes, a colorful history, and a diverse population all characterize the West. Students can celebrate this region in an original song.

Choose a Melody

Week 1

👥👥 whole class   🕐 15 minutes

Materials: chalkboard

Tell the students they are going to celebrate the West by writing their own original song lyrics about the region. They will use the tune of a well-known song and write new words to go with the music. Then hold a brainstorming session with the whole class to list songs they know on the chalkboard. The songs they suggest should be familiar to most of the class, have rhyming lyrics, and be easy to sing. Here are some possibilities to consider: "Oh! Susanna," "On Top of Old Smoky," "Clementine," "Red River Valley," "She'll Be Comin' 'Round the Mountain," and "Home on the Range." After students have suggested all the songs they can think of, invite them to vote for a song to use as a base for their new lyrics.

Choose a Topic

Week 2

👥👥 group   🕐 20 minutes

Materials: note cards, pencils

Form small groups. Explain to the class that each group will write one verse for the class song, "Song of the West."

Invite the groups to think of three aspects of the West. Have them write each idea on a separate note card. On the back of each card, each group member should write his or her name. When you have collected all the cards, organize them so that each group gets one of its choices, but no two groups are given the same idea to write about.

Here are some ideas students might use: The Rocky Mountains, Yellowstone National Park, Alaska, Death Valley, the Central Valley, the Gold Rush, the film industry, European explorers, the Wild West.

© Scott Foresman 4

Write the Words

🚶🚶 group   🕐 45 minutes

Materials: paper, pencils

Working together in their groups, students can now write their verses for the song. Each group should appoint a recorder to write down the final version. Encourage students to write rhyming lyrics, but rhyme should not be required. However, the words must scan, or fit the rhythm of the song, so that they can be sung easily by the class. Collect the verses after all the groups have completed their work. Type or write the verses in an order of your choosing, and insert the title "Song of the West." Make copies to hand out to each student.

Sing Out!

🚶🚶 group   🕐 20 minutes

Materials: copies of "Song of the West"

Give each student a copy of "Song of the West." Invite each group to sing its verse for the class. Then have all the students join in and sing the whole song together.

© Scott Foresman 4

Shooting the West

Filmmakers are planning a documentary movie about the West—its land, people, and history. What should be in the film? How will they decide? Time for a meeting!

The Parts: (5 players)
- Film Director
- Terry
- Sam
- Kim
- Sandy

Director's Notes: This is a play with a film director and four filmmakers. Players will memorize their parts. Sometimes they will improvise, or make up, their lines. With your group, brainstorm what players might say about what should be in a film about the land, people, and history of the West.

Tell your players to watch for stage directions in the play. They are given in parentheses.

Film Director:	OK, people. I want this film to show the *real* West. Any ideas?
Terry:	There are so many different kinds of scenery in the West. We should show _____. *Improv Directions: Tell about showing beautiful and interesting scenes in the West. Don't mention Alaska.)*
Sam:	Don't forget Alaska. That's part of the West, too. We should show _____. **(Improv Directions:** *Tell about showing scenes in Alaska.)*
Kim:	What about Hawaii? **(Improv Directions:** *Tell about showing scenes in Hawaii.)*
Film Director:	*(pretending to take notes)* Let's talk about what will *happen* in the movie. Let's start with "you are there" scenes from history?
Sandy:	Yes. We should have something about Juan Rodríguez Cabrillo, the Portuguese explorer. *(Talk about Cabrillo.)*

Theater Talk

documentary: a film of fact, not fiction

screenplay: a script, or the written words, for a movie

© Scott Foresman 4

Terry:	After Cabrillo, why don't we jump ahead to 1840 and the Gold Rush?
Sam:	Right. We could show when James Marshall and John Sutter discover gold on the American River. *(**Improv Directions:** Tell about how the Gold Rush began.)*
Kim:	How about showing some kids in a Wild West town?
Film Director:	Sounds good.
Sandy:	We could also pretend to interview some famous people from the West.
Film Director:	I like that idea. Any suggestions?
Terry:	How about Levi Strauss? Everyone likes a success story.
Sam:	Let's interview a cowboy. We should show how hard their lives really were.
Kim:	We should also do a real interview with someone from a Tlingit family. Today the Tlingit live in modern villages, but they keep many of their old traditions.
Film Director:	This is a good start. We'll need to write the screenplay and hire actors and a crew. Then we'll be ready to shoot!
All:	*(Sigh, hold your heads, and indicate in other ways that you know you have a lot of work ahead of you.)* Let's get to work!

© Scott Foresman 4

Scenes from the Past

**Some of our nation's most colorful history comes from the West, and good history makes good documentaries.
Let's begin at the beginning.**

The Parts: (9 players)
- Narrator
- Sailor 1
- Sailor 2
- John Sutter
- Jane
- Juan Rodríguez Cabrillo
- James Marshall
- Martha
- Jess

Director's Notes: This is a section of a documentary about the West. It shows three scenes—Cabrillo sighting the California Coast, Marshall and Sutter discovering gold, and children living in a town in the Wild West. The narrator, in voice-over, lets the movie audience know when a new scene is starting. You may want to keep the narrator out of the view of your audience.

Players will memorize their parts. Sometimes they will improvise, or make up, their lines. With your group, brainstorm what players might say in each scene.

Narrator: Let's join Juan Rodríguez Cabrillo and his crew. The year is 1542. They are sailing up the coast of what we now call California.

Sailor 1: I think we'll find great riches—like silver and gold! *(Improv Directions: Talks about becoming wealthy.)*

Cabrillo: Remember, our orders are to find a water route to the Atlantic Ocean.

Sailor 2: I hear that people from Spain want to come and live here.

Sailor 1: I'd rather return to Portugal—as a wealthy man.

Cabrillo: Who knows? We will continue our voyage, and see what we find.

Narrator: Cabrillo died in 1543, but his crew sailed on. People from Spain did settle in California—as did people from many other places. *(Cabrillo and Sailors exit stage left. Sutter and Marshall enter stage right.)* Now we move ahead. The year is 1848. James Marshall and John Sutter are about to make a very exciting discovery along the American River in California.

Sutter:	Hi, Marshall. How's the work on my sawmill?
Marshall:	Just fine. But I've been seeing some shiny stuff in the water. Look—there's some of it now! *(Points.)*
Sutter:	I think that's gold, Marshall! Nuggets of gold! *(**Improv Directions:** Talks about keeping the discovery a secret.)*
Marshall:	*(**Improv Directions:** Talks about what he and Sutter should do when they're rich.)*
Narrator:	Word did get out, and it spread quickly. Thousands came, but many did not find gold. Instead, they settled in the Central Valley and became farmers and ranchers. *(Sutter and Marshall exit stage left. Martha, Jane, and Jess enter stage right.)* Now let's move forward a little—to the Wild West.
Martha:	*(pointing to a poster)* Hey, look. Buffalo Bill's Wild West show is coming to town!
Jane:	My mama says if I'm really good, I can go to see it.
Jess:	My cousin saw the show last year. She said *(**Improv Directions:** Talks about what he has heard about the show).*
Martha:	My papa says what we need around here is less shooting and better policing!
Narrator:	The Wild West was tamed by the 1890s. But the legends still live on in stories, songs, and, of course, movie Westerns.

© Scott Foresman 4

Unit 6
Drama PLAY

Let's Talk West

Documentary interviews can tell us a lot about history. Go straight to some westerners to learn about the West.

The Parts: (6 players)
- Pedro
- Joshua
- Beth
- Cowboy
- Levi Strauss
- Tlingit Woman

Director's Notes: This is a section of a documentary about the West. It shows three interviews with characters from the West.

Players will memorize their parts. Sometimes they will improvise, or make up, their lines. With your group, go over the script and brainstorm with players how they might answer the questions they will be asked.

Pedro:	What do you do for a living?
Cowboy:	I'm a cowboy.
Pedro:	What does that mean?
Cowboy:	I work on a ranch in Montana, and I drive cattle to railroad towns. *(Improv Directions: Add information about why cattle are taken to railroad towns.)*
Pedro:	Do you like your job?
Cowboy:	Yep, I like it. But it can get pretty lonely. Sometimes I go for months without seeing anyone except the guys I work with.
Pedro:	What do you do on the ranch?
Cowboy:	Just about everything—pitch hay, clear land, fix fences. But mainly I take care of the cattle while they're grazing on the range.
Pedro:	Well, thanks a lot for talking to us. *(Pedro and Cowboy exit. Joshua and Levi Strauss enter.)*
Joshua:	Would you tell us your name, please?
Strauss:	Certainly. I am Levi Strauss.
Joshua:	Almost everyone wears blue jeans these days. Some people call blue jeans "Levi's." Does that have anything to do with you?

Theater Talk

enter: come onto the stage

exit: leave the stage

© Scott Foresman 4

Strauss: It certainly does. I invented blue jeans. *(**Improv Directions:** Add information about making tough pants for miners during the California Gold Rush.)*

Joshua: Were you born in the United States?

Strauss: No. I was born in Germany. I came to this country in 1847.

Strauss: Would you call yourself a success?

Strauss: I certainly would. *(**Improv Directions:** Talks about what made his business a success.)*

Joshua: Thank you, Mr. Strauss. It's been very interesting talking to you. *(Joshua and Levi Strauss exit. Beth and Tlingit Woman enter.)*

Beth: Tell us a little about yourself.

Woman: I'm a member of the Tlingit tribe. I live in Alaska.

Beth: Do you still keep Tlingit traditions from the past?

Woman: My family lives in a modern village, but we do keep some of our old traditions. For example, we make beautiful Chilkat blankets. *(**Improv Directions:** Talks about how Chilkat blankets are made.)*

Beth: What's a potlatch?

Woman: It's a big party with lots of food where lots of presents are given. We still have potlatches. *(**Improv Directions:** Describes potlatch.)*

Beth: One more question. What can you tell us about the Sealaska Corporation?

Woman: *(**Improv Directions:** Talks about the Sealaska Corporation.)*

Beth: Thank you very much for talking with us.

Woman: You're welcome. *(Tlingit woman exits)*

Beth: All these people and their rich diversity have many wanting to "Go West!"

Short-Term Projects

Majestic mountains and breathtaking views are a few of the splendors of the West. The following projects will help your students celebrate the West's natural beauty.

Midwest Art Gallery

👤 individual   🕐 20 minutes

Materials: paper; crayons, markers, or paints and paintbrushes

Invite students to choose aspects of the West that capture their interest. They may choose historical events, such as the discovery of gold at Sutter's Mill or Cabrillo's sail up the Pacific coast. Or they may choose the landscape of the Rocky Mountains, Old Faithful, the rain forests of Hawaii, the redwoods of California, or the Mojave Desert. They might even choose recreational activities, such as surfing in Hawaii or in Southern California. Have students draw or paint pictures of the topics they have chosen. Use a bulletin board as an "art gallery" to display the pictures. The "show" can be titled "Scenes from the West."

Rocky Mountain Field Guide

👥 group   🕐 45 minutes

Materials: paper, pencils, crayons or markers, research materials about animals

Students have learned that many animals live in the Rocky Mountains. Mountain goats and bighorn sheep live there above the timberline. Black bears and grizzly bears, mountain lions, elk, and mink live in the forests. Chipmunks, coyotes, and moose live in the valleys. The mountain streams are filled with fish. Encourage students to find out more about these animals. Invite students to work in small groups to choose animals to research, draw, and write about. Students may bind their group's pages together to create a "Field Guide to Animals of the Rockies."

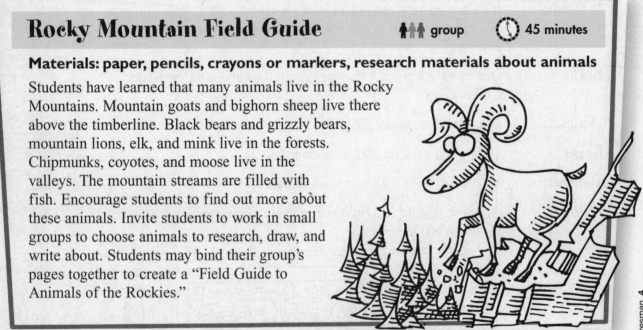

© Scott Foresman 4

Product Maps

partners **30 minutes**

Materials: paper, pencils, blackline master (page 139)

Invite students to make product maps of the states of the West.

1. Students first label each state on the blackline master outline map of the West on page 139. (Washington, Oregon, California, Idaho, Nevada, Montana, Wyoming, Utah, Colorado, Alaska, and Hawaii).

2. Students refer to their textbooks and an encyclopedia to make a list of the products that come from each state.

3. Students create symbols to represent each product they have listed.

4. Students draw symbols on their maps to show where the products are grown or produced.

Remember! Keep working on that Long-Term Project.

Tundra Dioramas

partners **20 minutes**

Materials: paper, pencils, crayons or markers; shoe boxes; tape; scissors

Students have read about the climate and landscape of the Alaskan tundra—a cold, flat area where trees cannot grow. They have learned that this is the area where the Iditarod is held. Together list animals that live in the Alaskan tundra. Mention that the arctic hare, the arctic wolf, the polar bear, and the arctic fox blend in with the snow because their fur is white. Other animals include musk oxen, seals, and walruses. Invite students to create dioramas of the Alaskan tundra. They can include animals or even a dogsled race.

Model Mountains

group **30 minutes**

Materials: cardboard, clay or home-made play dough

Several mountain ranges rise in the West, for example the Rocky Mountains, the Sierra Nevadas, and the Cascades. Mount McKinley, the nation's tallest mountain, is in Alaska. Invite students to view the photographs of the mountains of the West in the textbook. Then they can make their own model mountains out of clay. Students should build their clay mountains on bases of cardboard. They can display their mountains together to make a model mountain range.

Writing Projects

**Mountains. Forests. Volcanoes. The West has a lot to inspire
students to express themselves through writing.**

What Makes a Volcano Erupt?

Students have learned that there are several active volcanoes
in the West, including Mount Saint Helens and the volcanoes
of Hawaii. On page 377 of the textbook, they can find an
explanation of what makes a volcano erupt. Invite students
to write cause-and-effect paragraphs in their own words that
explain this natural phenomenon. Remind them to write
clearly and logically.

Mountain Haiku

Review with students that a haiku poem is a short, simple, unrhymed poem—only
three lines. The number of syllables in each line is not strictly set, but the first and last
lines should be shorter than the middle one. Also review with students that haiku
poetry originated in Japan and that it usually focuses on observations of nature. As an
example, write on the chalkboard the following haiku by the seventeenth-century
Japanese poet Matsuo Basho:

> old pond...
> a frog leaps in
> water's sound

Encourage students to look at photographs of western mountains in the textbook.
Invite them to write their own haikus, inspired by these mountain scenes. Students may
share their haikus in a class reading.

Yellowstone Journal

Ask students to research the natural attractions (mountains, canyons, waterfalls,
geysers, and hot springs) and animals of Yellowstone National Park. Invite students to
suppose they could spend a day in Yellowstone Park. In journal entries, students should
note their thoughts and impressions as well as what they did and what they saw.

Western Cookery

Invite students to peruse cookbooks at home or in class to find recipes for dishes made with products of the West—for example, apple pie, pineapple upside-down cake, beef stew, grape jam. Invite them to write recipes for one or more of these dishes in their own words. Students may combine their recipes in a class cookbook called "New West Cuisine."

Portrait of the Sierra Nevadas

Direct students' attention to the painting, *The Grand Canyon of the Yellowstone,* by Thomas Moran, on page 361 of the textbook. Suggest they take a few minutes to look over the painting and take in its details. Invite students to write descriptions of the scene in the painting. Remind them that descriptive writing should contain vivid adjectives that will help the reader "see" what the writer is describing. Tell students that Thomas Moran was one of the greatest American landscape painters. He is famous for his paintings of the American West. His paintings gave people their first views of places that later became national parks.

North and South: Compare and Contrast

Students have read that California has more than one type of climate. The northern part of the state is cool most of the year, with a good deal of rainfall, while the southern part of the state is warm and sunny. Invite students to write paragraphs comparing and contrasting the climates in the northern and southern parts of California. They might include activities that are appropriate for the two different climates.

Citizenship

Caring

We all have problems, but it's a lonely world for people who care only about themselves! Here are some activities to heighten students' awareness of the importance of caring.

Talk briefly with the class about the importance of caring about others. Lead students to understand that caring for each other means we're not alone. It means that when we have problems, we can count on the support of others to help us get through our difficulties. And if we want that kind of support from others, we should be willing to give it. That's what community is all about.

Present students with this scenario: A new student enters the class in the middle of the year. He or she does not know anyone and seems a little shy. What would be a caring response? (A caring person might eat lunch with the new student or invite the student to join in an after-school activity.)

Discuss with students how to know what to do when friends have problems. Bring out in discussion that putting one "in someone else's shoes" often helps. A person may ask himself or herself, "If I were in this situation, how would I want someone to help me?" A person may also use brainstorming with a friend as a problem-solving technique. He or she might ask, "What is wrong? What can we do about it?"

Important: Let students know that sometimes a friend's problem may be too serious or too difficult for another young person to help with. In such cases, he or she should strongly encourage the friend to speak to his or her family, teacher, or some other adult who will be able to offer help and support. It's important that children not consider themselves responsible for solving every problem another person may have.

Invite students to extend the activity by writing a response to the two situations presented in the blackline master worksheet on page 133. Have them respond by suggesting ways that a caring person would act in each situation.

© Scott Foresman 4

Dare to Care

When a friend has a problem, how do you show that you care? Read each of the problems. Write about what you would do to show that you care.

Your friend is in charge of the class hamster. One day, she leaves the cage open and the hamster runs away. She tells you that she doesn't want your teacher to find out.

_____

_____

_____

_____

_____

_____

_____

When sides are chosen for basketball, your friend always gets picked last. He tells you that he doesn't want to play sports anymore.

_____

_____

_____

_____

_____

_____

_____

Short-Term Projects

**From totem poles to blue jeans—there's so much to learn about the West.
Enrich students' learning with these exciting projects.**

Totem Pole Stories

♦ individual   🕐 20 minutes

Materials: paper, pencils, crayons or markers

Students have learned that Tlingit families often placed totem poles outside their homes. The images, which are painted with bright colors, tell stories about the family's history. Invite students to choose characters they've encountered in books, movies, television shows, or folktales and design totem poles that tell stories about those characters. Encourage students to present their designs to the class, explaining how the images they've drawn relate to their characters' stories.

Songs of the Cowboys

👫👤 group   🕐 30 minutes

Materials: copies of song lyrics

Give students copies of song lyrics from "Home on the Range" and "Git Along, Little Dogies," two well-known folk songs about cowboys. Invite them to learn the tunes and the words so that they can sing the songs for the class. If they prefer, they can give choral readings of the lyrics. The complete lyrics can be found on the Internet or in songbooks. (Note: Explain to students that in "Git Along, Little Dogies," a *dogie* is a calf.)

"Go West" Bumper Stickers

👫 partners   🕐 20 minutes

Materials: paper, crayons or markers

If you're looking for recreation, the West has something for just about everyone—skiing, swimming, surfing, fishing, and more. Invite students to create bumper stickers to let people know of the West's many opportunities for recreation. Partners should work together to come up with catchy rhymes or slogans as well as visual images for their stickers.

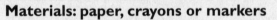

© Scott Foresman 4

Social Studies Plus!

Filling Needs

group 👨‍👩‍👧 🕐 20 minutes

Materials: paper, pencils

Miners needed pants that were made of tough material, that would last a long time, and that had a lot of pockets to carry tools. So Levi Strauss invented blue jeans. Blue jeans were a good idea because they filled a real need.

Mention to students other products that are successful because they fill needs—a backpack with wheels, for example. Then invite students to brainstorm new products to fill today's needs. Suggest they start with a list of needs and then come up with products to fill them.

Beautiful Blankets

🧍 individual 🕐 20 minutes

Materials: paper, pencils, crayons or markers

The Tlingit still make beautiful blankets called Chilkat blankets. Decorated with patterns and shapes of animals, traditional Chilkat blankets tell stories through the images woven into them. Invite students to make designs for their own blankets. Each blanket should tell a story, but it does not have to look like an authentic Chilkat blanket. Students should simply aim to create pleasing and colorful designs.

History Time Lines

👫 partners 🕐 20 minutes

Materials: paper, pencils, tape

Have students make "History of the West" time lines with Juan Cabrillo's voyage as the first event and Hawaii's statehood in 1959 as the last. Suggest that they begin by listing all the events they wish to include. Students can tape sheets of paper together to make their time lines. They should calibrate their time lines in one-hundred-year increments, beginning with the year 1500 and ending with the year 2000.

Remember! Keep working on that Long-Term Project.

Writing Projects

West begins with W. Invite students to investigate the other five W's of the West—who, what, when, where, and why—in writing.

Compare and Contrast Cities

Encourage students to revisit the discussions of Seattle, Washington, and Salt Lake City, Utah, in the textbook. Invite them to write paragraphs comparing and contrasting the two cities. You may suggest that they begin with a chart listing details about the two cities that are similar and different. Remind students that a paragraph should begin with a topic sentence stating the main idea and that other sentences in the paragraph should support that main idea.

Messages from L.A.

Challenge students to research the modern city of Los Angeles, California. Then ask them to suppose they are on vacation in L.A. and to write postcards or e-mail messages to friends telling what they are doing there and in the surrounding area. They may want to write about visits to such popular tourist attractions as Universal Studios, Disneyland, the Hollywood Walk of Fame, the beach at Santa Monica, or the Los Angeles County Art Museum.

Plan a Potlatch Party

Students have learned that the Tlingit still hold traditional parties called potlatches. At a potlatch, there is lots of food, music, and dancing. The host gives lots of gifts to all the guests. Invite students to write plans for a potlatch-style class party. What kinds of food will they have? What music will they play? What kind of dancing will there be? There must be gifts for everyone. What should they be?

Tell a Tall Tale

Cowboys liked to tell tall tales—exaggerated stories about things that could never really happen. It was said that Pecos Bill, for example, was a big and wild cowboy who lassoed his prey with a rattlesnake while riding atop a mountain lion. Invite students to make up their own original Wild West tales with cowboy heroes of their own creation.

Wild West Mayor

Students have learned that some of the towns in the Wild West—especially the "cow towns" where cowboys ended their trail drives—were wild and lawless places without effective law enforcement. Invite each student to imagine that he or she is the campaign manager for a candidate for mayor of a town in the Wild West. Have the students write campaign speeches in which the candidate tells the voters what he or she will do to bring law and order to the town. Mention to students that their solutions should be non-violent.

Gold Rush Skits

When gold was discovered in California, thousands of people came there, hoping to find gold and get rich. Some succeeded, but many more did not. Suggest that students revisit the discussion of the Gold Rush in the textbook. Invite them to write skits in which the characters are people involved in the Gold Rush. Remind students to write their skits in play form and to include stage directions in parentheses where needed.

Citizenship

Fairness

Is it always clear what is "fair" when people disagree? Students will give fairness some serious thought as they play "You Be the Judge."

Mayor Thomas Bradley judged the transportation system in Los Angeles unfair, because it favored people with cars. He helped create the Metro Rail to make it easier for everyone to get around the city.

Present this situation to students: There is enough money in the school budget to pay for only one basketball team, but both the boys and the girls want a team. What can be done so that no one is left out? Lead students to see that a compromise may be necessary to ensure fairness—perhaps a fund-raiser or a mixed team is possible.

Invite students to play "You Be the Judge." In the following disputes, students will tell why the situation is unfair and recommend changes to make it fairer.

1. **Good Time, Bad Time:** Two candidates are running for mayor. Each one has been granted an hour to give a campaign speech on the radio. The first candidate's speech is scheduled for 6:00 P.M. on Wednesday. The second candidate's speech is scheduled for 6:00 A.M. on Saturday. No other times are available. *(Possible solutions: The candidates could share both times, or they could give shorter speeches by splitting the Wednesday time and giving up the Saturday time.)*

2. **Walking the Dog:** Two children split a job walking a neighbor's dog. One walks the dog on Monday, Wednesday, and Friday, and the other walks the dog on Tuesday and Thursday. The neighbor pays each the same amount per week. *(Possible solutions: The children could take turns, each working two days or three days on alternate weeks, or the child who walks the dogs three times a week could receive extra pay.)*

3. **The Noisy Pool:** Two families live next door to each other. One family has a backyard swimming pool. They give lots of pool parties, where they make a lot of noise, starting in the afternoon and lasting late into the night. *(Possible solutions: The family with the pool agrees to be quiet after an agreed-upon time, or the family next door gives a schedule of when they will not be home and therefore not be bothered by the parties.)*

Social Studies Plus!

Product Map

Write the name of each state of the West on the blank lines. Then draw symbols on each state to show the products that come from that state.

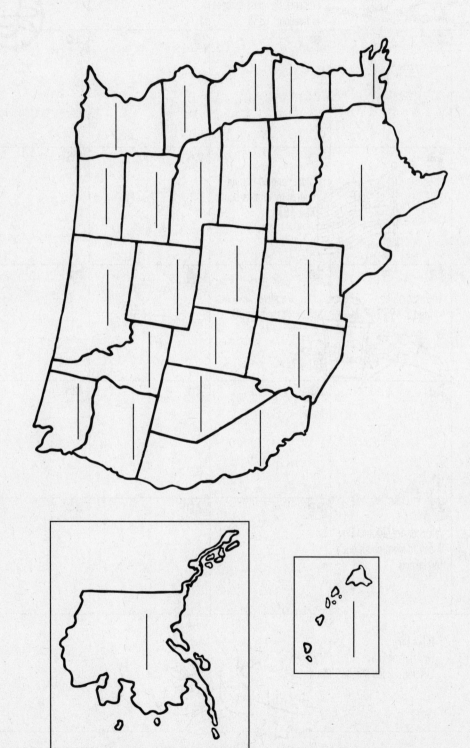

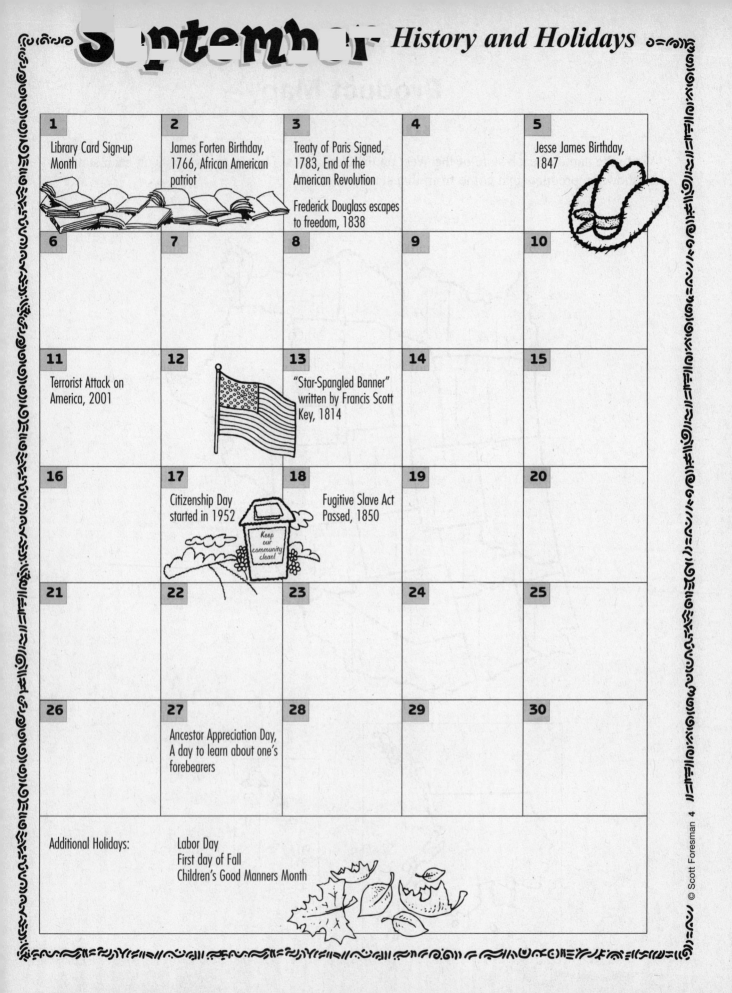

1 Library Card Sign-up Month	**2** James Forten Birthday, 1766, African American patriot	**3** Treaty of Paris Signed, 1783, End of the American Revolution Frederick Douglass escapes to freedom, 1838	**4**	**5** Jesse James Birthday, 1847
6	**7**	**8**	**9**	**10**
11 Terrorist Attack on America, 2001	**12**	**13** "Star-Spangled Banner" written by Francis Scott Key, 1814	**14**	**15**
16	**17** Citizenship Day started in 1952	**18** Fugitive Slave Act Passed, 1850	**19**	**20**
21	**22**	**23**	**24**	**25**
26	**27** Ancestor Appreciation Day, A day to learn about one's forebearers	**28**	**29**	**30**

Additional Holidays:
Labor Day
First day of Fall
Children's Good Manners Month

Keep our community clean!

© Scott Foresman 4

October *History and Holidays*

1	**2**	**3**	**4**	**5** Tecumseh Death Anniversary, 1813
6	**7**	**8**	**9**	**10**
11	**12** Columbus Day	**13** White House cornerstone laid, 1792 "Molly Pitcher" Birthday, 1754, American Revolution heroine	**14**	**15**
16 Dictionary Day, Noah Webster Birthday, 1758 World Food Day John Brown's Raid, 1859	**17**	**18**	**19** Yorktown Victory, 1781	**20**
21	**22**	**23**	**24** United Nations Day	**25**
26 Erie Canal Opens, 1825	**27** Theodore Roosevelt Birthday, 1858, 26th president	**28** Statue of Liberty Dedication at New York Harbor, 1886	**29**	**30**
31 Halloween	Additional Holidays	Diversity Awareness Month		

November — History and Holidays

1	2 Daniel Boone Birthday, 1734	3 Sandwich Day, Invented by John Montague, 1718	4	5
6	7	8	9 Benjamin Banneker Birthday, 1731, Helped design Wash., D.C.	10
11 Veterans Day	12 Elizabeth Cady Stanton Birthday, 1815	13	14 Nellie Bly goes around the world in 72 days, 1889	15
16 United Nations International Day for Tolerance	17	18	19 Lincoln's Gettysburg Address, 1863	20
21	22	23	24	25
26 Sojourner Truth Death Anniversary, 1883	27	28	29	30 Mark Twain Birthday, 1835

Additional Holidays:

National Geography Awareness Week
General Election Day
Thanksgiving Day, 4th Thursday of the month
American Indian Heritage Month

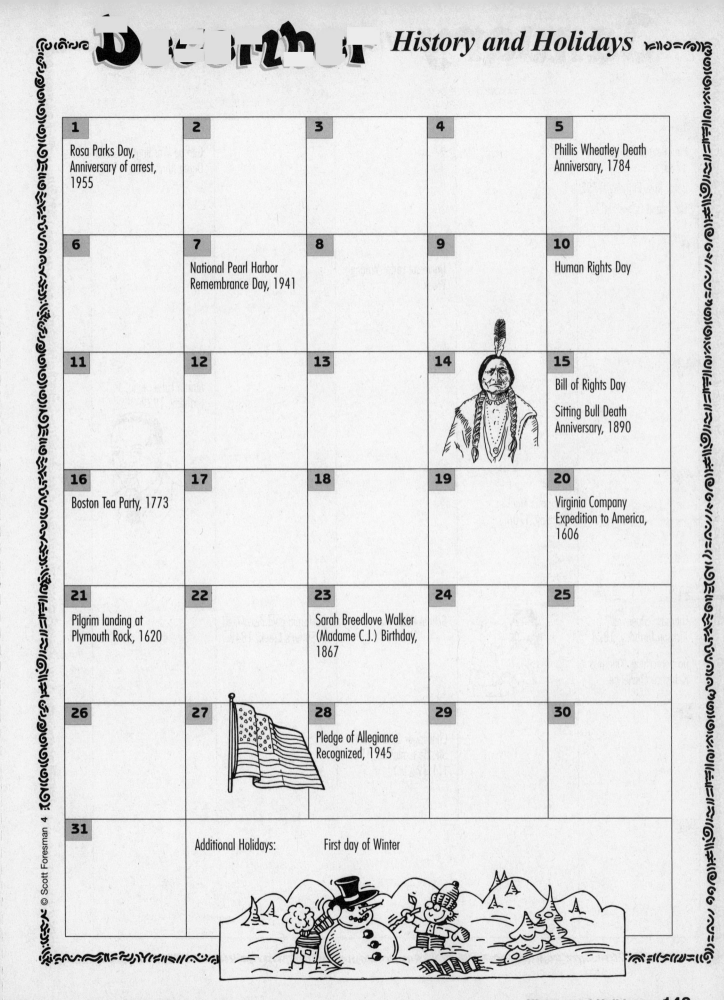

1 Rosa Parks Day, Anniversary of arrest, 1955	**2**	**3**	**4**	**5** Phillis Wheatley Death Anniversary, 1784
6	**7** National Pearl Harbor Remembrance Day, 1941	**8**	**9**	**10** Human Rights Day
11	**12**	**13**	**14**	**15** Bill of Rights Day Sitting Bull Death Anniversary, 1890
16 Boston Tea Party, 1773	**17**	**18**	**19**	**20** Virginia Company Expedition to America, 1606
21 Pilgrim landing at Plymouth Rock, 1620	**22**	**23** Sarah Breedlove Walker (Madame C.J.) Birthday, 1867	**24**	**25**
26	**27**	**28** Pledge of Allegiance Recognized, 1945	**29**	**30**
31	Additional Holidays:	First day of Winter		

1 Paul Revere Birthday, 1735 Betsy Ross Birthday, 1752 Ellis Island Opens, 1892	**2**	**3**	**4**	**5** George Washington Carver Death Anniversary, 1943
6	**7**	**8** Universal Letter Writing Week	**9**	**10**
11	**12**	**13**	**14**	**15** Martin Luther King, Jr. Birthday, 1929
16	**17** Benjamin Franklin Birthday, 1706	**18**	**19**	**20**
21 Thomas "Stonewall" Jackson Birthday, 1824 Do Something: Kindness & Justice Challenge	**22**	**23** School Nurse Day	**24** California gold discovered in Sutter's Creek, 1848	**25**
26	**27**	**28** Challenger Space Shuttle Explosion, 1986 (11:39 A.M.)	**29**	**30**
31				

February History and Holidays

1 Langston Hughes Birthday, 1902	**2** Groundhog Day	**3**	**4** Charles Lindbergh, Birthday, 1902, First to fly solo across the Atlantic	**5**
6 "Babe" Ruth Birthday, 1895	**7** Laura Ingalls Wilder Birthday, 1867, *Little House on the Prairie* author	**8**	**9**	**10** French and Indian War Ends, 1763, Treaty of Paris
11 Thomas Alva Edison Birthday, 1847, Inventor	**12** Abraham Lincoln Birthday, 1809	**13**	**14** Valentine's Day	**15**
16	**17**	**18**	**19**	**20**
21	**22** George Washington Birthday, 1732	**23**	**24**	**25**
26	**27**	**28**		

Additional Holidays: Black History Month Presidents' Day

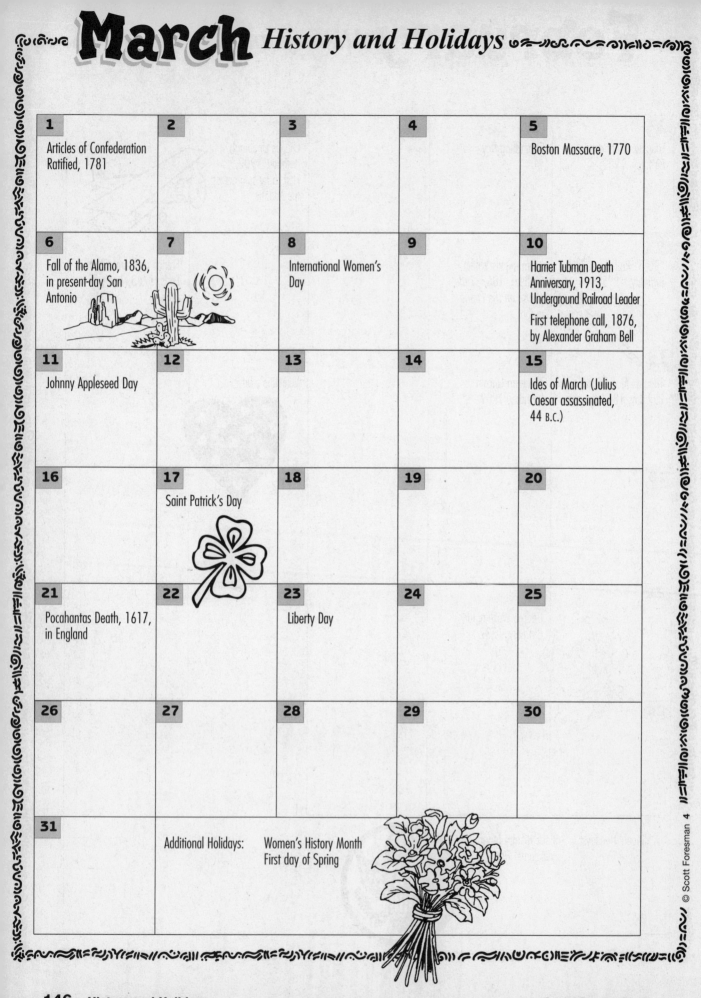

1 Articles of Confederation Ratified, 1781	**2**	**3**	**4**	**5** Boston Massacre, 1770
6 Fall of the Alamo, 1836, in present-day San Antonio	**7**	**8** International Women's Day	**9**	**10** Harriet Tubman Death Anniversary, 1913, Underground Railroad Leader First telephone call, 1876, by Alexander Graham Bell
11 Johnny Appleseed Day	**12**	**13**	**14**	**15** Ides of March (Julius Caesar assassinated, 44 B.C.)
16	**17** Saint Patrick's Day	**18**	**19**	**20**
21 Pocahontas Death, 1617, in England	**22**	**23** Liberty Day	**24**	**25**
26	**27**	**28**	**29**	**30**
31	Additional Holidays:	Women's History Month First day of Spring		

© Scott Foresman 4

April *History and Holidays*

1 April Fools' Day	**2** International Children's Book Day	**3**	**4**	**5** Booker T. Washington Birthday, 1856
6	**7**	**8**	**9** Civil War Ends, 1865, Appomattox Courthouse	**10**
11 Civil Rights Act of 1968	**12** Polio Vaccine, 1955, Developed by Dr. Jonas E. Salk First Space Shuttle flight, Columbia, 1981	**13** Thomas Jefferson Birthday, 1743	**14** Moment of Laughter Day	**15**
16	**17**	**18** Paul Revere's "Midnight Ride," 1775	**19**	**20**
21	**22** Earth Day, 1970	**23**	**24**	**25** Take Our Daughters and Sons To Work Day
26 Arbor Day, National day for planting trees	**27** Ulysses Simpson Grant Birthday, 1822, 18th president	**28**	**29**	**30**

May *History and Holidays*

1 May Day, Work celebration Law Day	**2** Robert's Rules Day	**3**	**4**	**5** Cinco De Mayo, Mexico, Anniversary of Battle of Puebla, 1862
6	**7**	**8** No Socks Day, Make less laundry and help the environment	**9**	**10**
11	**12**	**13**	**14** Lewis and Clark Expedition, 1804 Jamestown, Virginia, founded, 1607	**15** National Bike to Work Day UN International Day of Families
16	**17** Sue exhibited in Chicago, 2000, largest and most complete Tyrannosaurus Rex ever discovered	**18**	**19**	**20** Homestead Act, 1862, Signed by President Lincoln
21 American Red Cross founded, 1881	**22**	**23**	**24** First telegraph message sent, 1844, by Samuel Morse	**25** First Constitutional Convention, Philadelphia, 1787
26	**27** Rachel Louise Carson Birthday, 1907	**28**	**29** John Fitzgerald Kennedy Birthday, 1917, 35th president	**30**
31	Additional Holidays:	National Family Week, 1st week in May Mother's Day, 2nd Sunday in May Memorial Day, Last Monday in May National Pet Week		

Social Studies Plus!

1	2	3	4	5
6 D-Day Anniversary, 1944 Susan B. Anthony fined for voting, 1872	**7**	**8**	**9**	**10**
11	**12**	**13** Northwest Ordinance, 1787	**14** Flag Day, Proclaimed 1916 Harriet Beecher Stowe Birthday, 1811, *Uncle Tom's Cabin* author	**15**
16	**17**	**18** Dr. Sally Ride, First American woman in space, 1983	**19** Juneteenth, 1868, News of the Emancipation Proclamation reached Texas	**20**
21	**22**	**23**	**24**	**25** Battle of Little Bighorn, Custer's Last Stand, 1876 Last Great Buffalo Hunt, 1882
26	**27** "Happy Birthday To You" composed, 1859	**28**	**29**	**30**

Additional Holidays: Father's Day / First day of Summer

1 First U.S. Zoo, 1874	**2** Thurgood Marshall Birthday, 1908	**3**	**4** "America the Beautiful" published, 1895 Independence Day, 1776 Stephen Foster Birthday, "Oh! Susanna" songwriter	**5** Phineas Taylor Barnum Birthday, 1810, Circus promoter
6	**7**	**8**	**9**	**10**
11 John Quincy Adams Birthday, 1767, 6th president	**12**	**13**	**14** Bastille Day, France, 1789 Woody Guthrie Birthday, 1912, "This Land Is Your Land" songwriter	**15**
16	**17** Opening Day at Disneyland, 1955, Anaheim, CA	**18**	**19** Woman's Rights Convention, Seneca Falls, 1848	**20** First Moon Walk, 1969
21	**22**	**23**	**24** Simon Bolivar Birthday, 1783	**25**
26	**27**	**28** Parents' Day	**29**	**30**
31				

© Scott Foresman 4

August History and Holidays

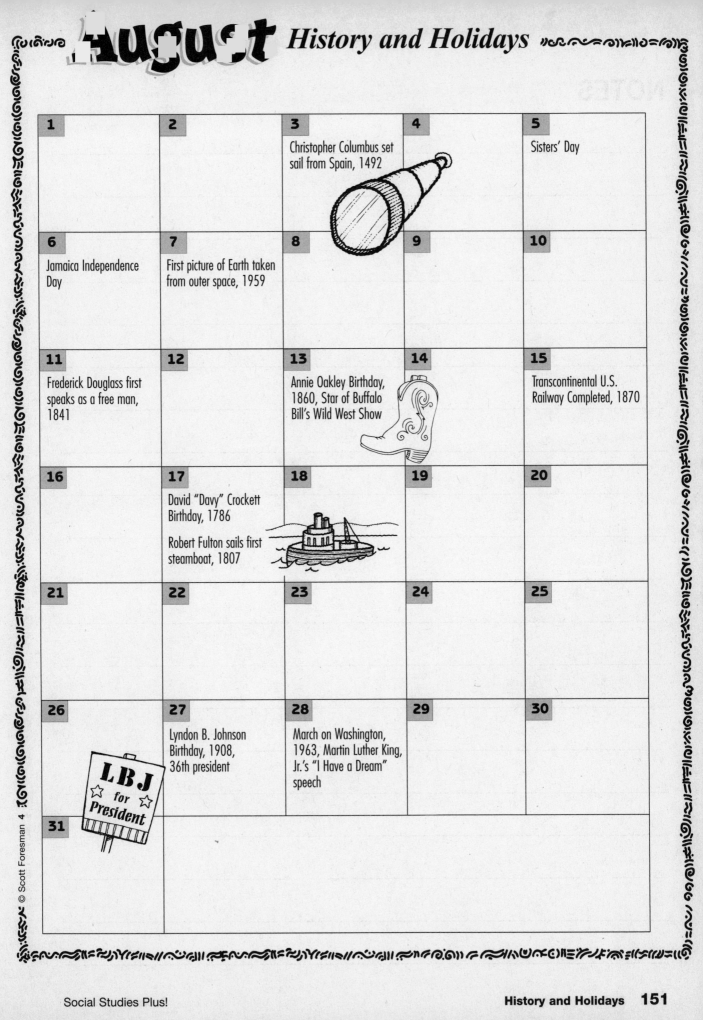

1	**2**	**3** Christopher Columbus set sail from Spain, 1492	**4**	**5** Sisters' Day
6 Jamaica Independence Day	**7** First picture of Earth taken from outer space, 1959	**8**	**9**	**10**
11 Frederick Douglass first speaks as a free man, 1841	**12**	**13** Annie Oakley Birthday, 1860, Star of Buffalo Bill's Wild West Show	**14**	**15** Transcontinental U.S. Railway Completed, 1870
16	**17** David "Davy" Crockett Birthday, 1786 Robert Fulton sails first steamboat, 1807	**18**	**19**	**20**
21	**22**	**23**	**24**	**25**
26	**27** Lyndon B. Johnson Birthday, 1908, 36th president	**28** March on Washington, 1963, Martin Luther King, Jr.'s "I Have a Dream" speech	**29**	**30**
31				

NOTES

NOTES

NOTES

NOTES

NOTES

NOTES

NOTES

NOTES

NOTES

NOTES

Social Studies Plus!